AF862391

An Investigation into the Management of Interest Rate Risk in Large UK Companies

Christine Helliar[1], Alpa Dhanani[2], Suzanne Fifield[1] and Lorna Stevenson[1]

[1]University of Dundee

[2]University of Cardiff

ELSEVIER

AMSTERDAM • BOSTON • HEIDELBERG • LONDON
NEW YORK • OXFORD • PARIS • SAN DIEGO
SAN FRANCISCO • SINGAPORE • SYDNEY • TOKYO

CIMA Publishing is an imprint of Elsevier

CIMA PUBLISHING

CIMA Publishing
An imprint of Elsevier
Linacre House, Jordan Hill, Oxford OX2 8DP
30 Corporate Drive, Burlington, MA 01803

First published 2005

Copyright © 2005, Christine Helliar, Alpa Dhanani, Suzanne Fifield and Lorna Stevenson. All rights reserved

The rights of Christine Helliar, Alpa Dhanani, Suzanne Fifield and Lorna Stevenson to be identified as the authors of this work has been asserted in accordance with the Copyright, Designs and Patents Act 1988

No part of this publication may be reproduced in any material form (including photocopying or storing in any medium by electronic means and whether or not transiently or incidentally to some other use of this publication) without the written permission of the copyright holder except in accordance with the provisions of the Copyright, Designs and Patents Act 1988 or under the terms of a licence issued by the Copyright Licensing Agency Ltd, 90 Tottenham Court Road, London, England W1T 4LP. Applications for the copyright holder's written permission to reproduce any part of this publication should be addressed to the publisher

Permissions may be sought directly from Elsevier's Science and Technology Rights Department in Oxford, UK: phone: (+44) (0) 1865 843830; fax: (+44) (0) 1865 853333; e-mail: permissions@elsevier.com. You may also complete your request on-line via the Elsevier homepage (http://www.elsevier.com), by selecting 'Customer Support' and then 'Obtaining Permissions'

British Library Cataloguing in Publication Data
A catalogue record for this book is available from the British Library

Library of Congress Cataloguing in Publication Data
A catalogue record for this book is available from the Library of Congress

ISBN 0 7506 6598 x

For information on all CIMA Publishing Publications
visit our website at www.cimapublishing.com

Typeset by Integra Software Services Pvt. Ltd, Pondicherry, India
www.integra-india.com
Printed and bound in Great Britain

Working together to grow
libraries in developing countries

www.elsevier.com | www.bookaid.org | www.sabre.org

ELSEVIER BOOK AID International Sabre Foundation

Contents

Acknowledgements

The authors would like to thank CIMA for their generous funding of this project. They would also like to thank all the busy businessmen and women who gave their time to be interviewed or to fill in the questionnaire survey, upon which this publication is based, and without whom this project would not have been possible.

Executive Summary

This monograph reports the findings of research that was carried out in 2002–2003 investigating the interest rate risk (IRR) management practices of UK firms. Risk has become very prevalent in society, and responsibility for the management of risk in the guise of corporate governance has hit the headlines after the scandals of Enron, Worldcom and Tyco. Financial risk has pre-dominated, with the use of special purpose vehicles to hide fraudulent financial transactions at Enron and accounting abuses elsewhere. Financial risk has also hit the headlines when derivatives transactions that are normally used to reduce, or hedge, risk do not work as anticipated, such as at Orange County and Gibsons Greetings, or have been used illegally by rogue traders such as at Barings by Nick Leeson and at Allied Irish Bank by John Rusnak.

The media's attention on the financial well-being of organisations spurred the authors to investigate a subject that appears to have been largely ignored in recent times; that of IRR management. This study examines nine key questions through the use of: (i) interviews with UK treasurers; and (ii) a questionnaire survey. In particular, the research questions ask whether IRR is

- important to all UK companies, irrespective of size;
- actively managed by UK companies, with the establishment of a clear IRR policy;
- important to companies with different equity, funding and gearing structures;
- dependent upon the same factors in all firms;
- more important than foreign exchange (FX) rate risk;
- managed differently depending upon forecasts of future interest rates, inflation rates, yield curve movements or a combination of factors;
- managed through the use of derivative products, especially interest rate swaps;
- monitored at board level such that corporate governance is maintained with effective monitoring, reporting and control guidelines;
- likely to change as the International Accounting Standards' environment changes.

The findings from this study confirm that IRR management is important to UK firms, but that larger firms have the resources to manage this risk on an active basis. Smaller firms have to prioritise making sure that their fundamental operations are effective before they have the time and resources to undertake treasury management. The larger UK firms that undertake active IRR management normally have clear goals and policies, with limits often set by the Board of Directors on the amount of funding that should be at fixed rates, and with established parameters for the gearing level. However, IRR management appears to be important to all companies, irrespective of their gearing level and financial standing. Often the IRR policy approved by Boards of Directors reflects their risk preferences and financial factors such as gearing, credit ratings and the existence of covenants.

Respondents to the questionnaire survey were asked their views about the management of interest rates in comparison with exchange rates, and the findings suggest that IRR management is more important to UK companies than FX rate risk.

The views of treasurers confirm that interest rate movements, the shape of the yield curve and other economic factors influence the actions that are taken about IRR management. For example, companies' IRR policies have a great deal of flexibility, and treasurers have a lot of freedom within these parameters for active risk management. Depending upon treasurers' views of the interest rate and inflationary environment, companies either fix the interest rates on their debt for the medium to long term or, alternatively, decide to keep their debt at mainly short-term floating rates of finance.

The companies that actively manage their IRR do so through a variety of means, but one of the most common methods is through the use of the derivatives market – especially the use of interest rate swaps. Treasurers do not like using futures or other exchange-traded instruments, but there is a common acceptance of the use of over-the-counter (OTC) products such as swaps for IRR management.

The recent scandals over the use of derivatives, and the focus on corporate governance may suggest that companies have implemented a strict regime of monitoring and control over treasury departments' activities. However, this does not appear to be so evident, with the monitoring, reporting and control process relying upon the appointment of dedicated professionals that are trusted to carry out the IRR policies as effectively as possible. Many companies have not adopted a frequent reporting pattern for their treasury departments to report at a Board of Director level, with some companies admitting that they report only once a year, and some claim that they never report to a Board committee at all.

This may all change with the imminent arrival of IAS 39, the International Accounting Standard for Derivatives, that will be in force by January 2005 for all EU companies. The topic of hedge accounting and the treatment of fair values may have a significant impact on many companies' reported profits, and the volatility of earnings is likely to increase. This study finds that there is a lot of discomfort with the implementation of IAS 39, and the current activities of treasurers may change as a result of this accounting standard.

The findings of this research have a number of policy implications for the government and regulators:

- **Bank of England's Monetary Policy Committee (MPC)**
  The decisions of this committee are vitally important to the financing activities of UK companies, and any *surprise* decisions can cause the future investment plans, and hence job creation opportunities for society, to be shelved or altered drastically. However, the MPC need to consider the whole economy, and thus companies should not create potential problems for themselves, if the MPC do decide to change rates, by structuring their debt, capital structure and risk management practices to facilitate such action.
- **Other Central Bank's interest rate decisions**
  Many UK companies have large operations overseas, and the funding for these activities is often carried out in currencies to match the currency of those countries. Any *surprise* decisions by these monetary authorities overseas may also cause hardship or force companies to abandon their planned investment activities.
- **The International Accounting Standards Board (IASB)**
  Many UK companies are very apprehensive about the implementation of IAS 39 in January 2005. The particular problem is the requirement for hedge accounting and the documentation and 'effectiveness' rules that will be introduced. Many companies

will change their current IRR management practices as a result of this standard. It is worrying when companies' practices and real cash flows are affected by the implementation of an accounting standard. Although some accounting standards can have a positive effect on companies' practices, IAS 39 is a particular case of where it could be harmful. The practice of companies' mitigating risk, and employing matching and hedging are useful tools, but companies may stop doing this because of an accounting standard. Perhaps the IASB should try to improve interest rate decision-making by working backwards from improved disclosure.

- **Government legislation and professional bodies' rules on corporate governance**
  The effectiveness of Board of Director control over the activities of treasury departments should be enhanced. Although many companies have very good procedures, some companies still appear to have very lax procedures over their financial risk management practices. Many companies do not actively involve the audit committee and the 'Best Practice' policies of professional associations including accountancy bodies such as CIMA or the Association of Corporate Treasurers (ACT) should address this issue.
- **Professional bodies**
  The professional bodies need to examine their training for both new recruits and their continuing professional development (CPD) programmes. New trainees, for example those taking their CIMA exams, should be rehearsed in basic IRR management skills which they could then apply, once professionally qualified, in the firms within which they may eventually work. Further, those that have qualified may need to keep up to date with the latest innovations and best practice recommendations. For example, CIMA members now have a fast-track route to qualify with the ACT, and these individuals may be responsible for the IRR management requirements of many large companies. Their professional expertise should be continually updated through a rigorous CPD programme.

In summary, this research has demonstrated that IRR management is of great importance to UK companies, and will hopefully assist UK companies and regulators in reducing this financial risk in the operations of UK companies.

This Page is Intentionally Left Blank

1

Interest Rate Risk Management

This Page is Intentionally Left Blank

1.1 Introduction

The management of interest rate risk (IRR) is important to many market players in the global community, and the growth in the interest rate derivatives market in the last decade demonstrates its increasing importance. For example, the Bank of England's 2001 triennial survey, in conjunction with the Bank for International Settlements, reported a dramatic increase in the volume of derivative trades in the over-the-counter (OTC) market; in particular, the survey highlighted that the interest rate derivatives market was a far larger and more important market than the currency derivatives market. For example, in the three years between 1998 and 2001, the global OTC derivatives market increased by 53 per cent to $580 billion per day. In addition, the survey revealed that in the UK the interest rate derivatives market grew by 93 per cent but, conversely, the currency derivatives market shrunk by 22 per cent (Bank of England Quarterly Bulletin, 2002).

1.2 Risk

The approach to risk adopted in this monograph follows the textbook view that equates risk with volatility; the more variable the possible outcomes, the higher the risk (Knight, 1921). Goodhart (1996) argued that financial volatility, which can have a detrimental effect on an organisation's operations, had five main causes. They were: (i) institutional change such as the collapse of the Bretton Woods agreement in 1973; (ii) de-regulation such as the lifting of interest rate controls; (iii) financial innovation, including derivatives; (iv) technology; and (v) globalisation. Since the 1980s and 1990s, all of these factors that cause financial volatility have been, and continue to be, present in the UK; companies are, therefore, having to cope with greater risks than they faced just a decade or two ago. Finnerty (1988) argues that the increase in market volatility and the frequency of tax and regulatory changes has stimulated financial innovation and has caused companies to try to lessen the financial constraints that they face; firms attempt to maximise their utility within a number of constraints imposed by governments, the markets and themselves. Finnerty also identifies eleven categories of financial innovation that have all increased the choice of products now available to organisational treasury departments to manage their financial risks.

1.3 Interest rate risk

Interest rate risk management is not purely about managing the interest line in the profit and loss account. It also encapsulates the management of the whole debt profile of the business, including the maturity of the debt, the currency of the debt, the fixed-floating mixture of the debt and expectations of future interest rates. IRR management in the UK has become a prominent feature in the corporate sector for four primary reasons.

First, the volatility of interest rates has increased considerably in recent years to record levels. This volatility is highlighted in Figure 1.1 which shows the level of short-term interest rates in the UK, France and Germany over the period 1987–2003. In particular, the figure shows that UK interest rates increased dramatically in the late 1980s before plunging to record lows in the twenty-first century. This volatility in interest rates in the last few decades has been a feature of not just the UK market, but international markets also. This increased volatility is highlighted further in Figure 1.2 which shows the movement in long-term

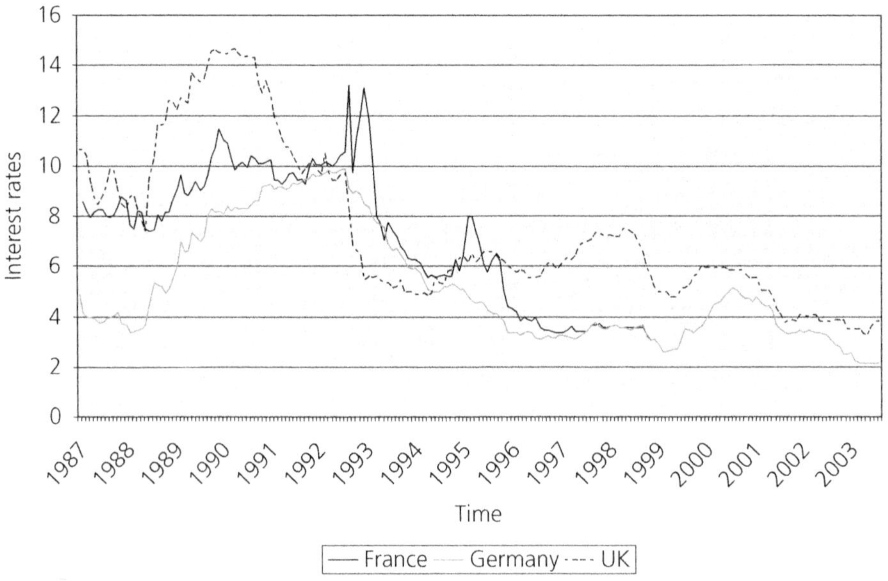

Figure 1.1 Short-term interest rates

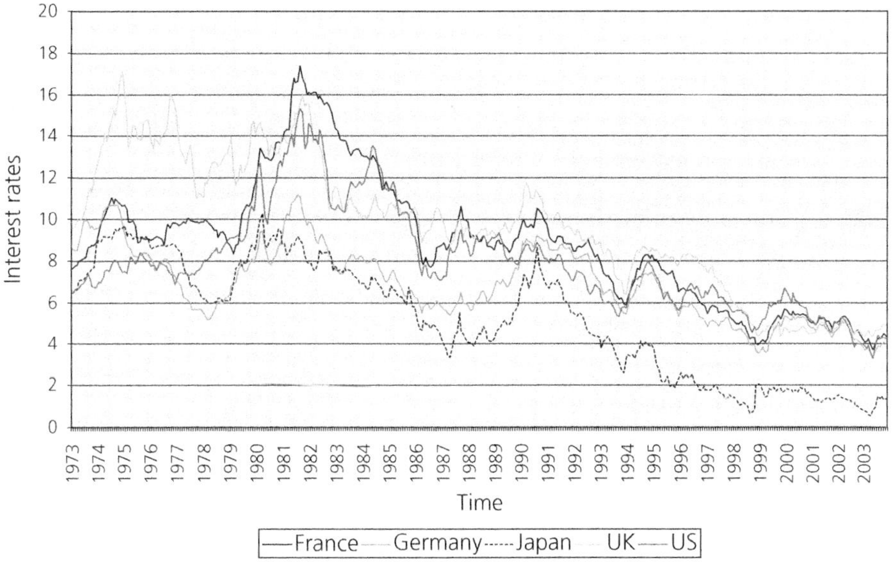

Figure 1.2 Long-term government bond yields

interest rates for the UK, US, France, Germany and Japan over the period 1973–2003. These wide fluctuations in interest rates can have a significant impact on the income streams and funding costs of firms; for example, a profitable project at one time may quite easily turn into an unprofitable project at another time (Helliar, 1997).

Second, the debt profile and gearing levels of firms has increased significantly due to a dramatic increase in the number of highly leveraged transactions such as management buy-outs and take-overs in the 1990s, that used substantial amounts of debt, such as mezzanine finance, to fund these deals. Moreover, there has been a general tendency for firms to finance more of their funding requirements through short-term and medium-term borrowing rather than through the use of equity finance. As a result, the debt profiles and gearing levels of firms have made them more vulnerable to changes in interest rates.

Third, lending institutions often use the interest coverage ratio and the gearing ratio as a basis for corporate funding, and lending covenants often refer to these factors in the legal documentation. Companies may, therefore, need to maintain these ratios within reasonable parameters and are thus required to manage their IRR. Finally, IRR management may be becoming more prevalent because international interest rates are converging, thereby reducing the natural hedging opportunities available from a portfolio of international exposures.

Consequently, the effect of interest rate movements on corporate borrowing and, in turn, on corporate performance has become of major significance for many companies. In turn, financial institutions and markets have responded by introducing a number of different derivative products to enable companies to manage their IRR (Helliar, 1997).

1.4 Interest rate risk management and derivatives usage

Many companies today often resort to derivative products such as swaps, options and forwards for risk management. There has been a proliferation in the use of these new and increasingly complex, financial instruments in recent years (Mallin, Ow-Yong and Reynolds, 2001). For example, just over twenty years ago the swaps market did not exist, whereas it is now one of the biggest and most important financial markets in the world (Helliar, 1997; Bank of England Quarterly Bulletin, 2001). As a result, many entities now utilise such instruments to transform their financial position, their reported performance and their risk profiles. This increase in derivatives usage has, in part, been attributed to the success of the finance industry in creating a variety of OTC and exchange-traded products (Froot, Scharfstein and Stein, 1993).

However, scandals at several well-known companies, which have been precipitated by the inappropriate use of derivatives, have prompted regulatory authorities to mandate disclosures by firms about the extent to which such financial instruments are employed. These regulatory measures have also been introduced to improve the corporate governance in organisations (Dunne *et al.*, 2004). In the UK, Financial Reporting Standard (FRS) 13 'Derivatives and other Financial Instruments: Disclosures' was adopted and became mandatory in March 1999. Financial risk management is currently subject to much debate, especially the accounting for derivative products, and a number of commentators are objecting to the introduction of International Accounting Standard (IAS) 39 'Financial Instruments: Recognition and Measurement' in its current form[1] (Horton and Macve, 2000). The impact of IAS 39 for the use of derivatives for IRR management may have important implications for UK companies.

Further, studies of corporate risk management have typically focused on the management of exchange rate risk (Belk and Glaum, 1990; Davis *et al.*, 1991; Marshall, 2000; Dhanani, 2001, 2003) while IRR management appears to have been largely neglected. This monograph tries to redress this balance by examining the IRR management practices of UK companies through the use of interviews and a questionnaire survey. These findings examine the views of corporate treasurers who are usually involved in the risk management strategies of their organisations and who have responsibility for implementing these strategies in practice.

1.5 Summary

This study seeks to examine the various approaches that organisations adopt to reduce the effect of financial volatility, especially changes in interest rates, on their cash flows and profits in order to reduce their financial risk. The remainder of the monograph is set out as follows. Chapter 2 provides a review of the literature and covers a variety of different aspects of risk management including the definitions of risk and IRR, a rationale for the corporate management of this risk, evidence of prior financial derivative practices and issues surrounding the control, monitoring and reporting of these derivatives. Chapter 3 discusses the research methods adopted in this study, while Chapters 4 and 5 document the findings from the interviews with corporate treasurers and the questionnaire survey of UK firms, respectively. An analysis of the techniques and products for IRR management highlights the complex operations undertaken by treasury departments in UK companies. Chapter 6 discusses the findings and offers a number of concluding observations.

---

[1]All EU-listed companies must comply with IAS 39 by 2005.

This Page is Intentionally Left Blank

2

Literature Review

This Page is Intentionally Left Blank

2.1 Introduction

Business plays a vital role in the current operation of UK society by providing jobs for the population and by producing goods and services that consumers wish to purchase. However, the risks that business organisations face have increased in both number and variety over the last few decades. The increase in competition, the globalisation of world markets, the rise of environmental concerns, the improvements in technology and the development of communication strategies have all added to the growth in risk which businesses face (Cobb, Helliar and Innes, 1995).

Risk has become an increasingly important topic over the last few years for many participants in business and finance, and concern has grown about the levels and complexity of risk in various financial and product markets. As a result of increased risk, several reports have been published by committees sponsored by the Stock Exchange (Cadbury, 1992; Turnbull, 1999), professional bodies (The Institute of Chartered Accountants in England and Wales, ICAEW, 1999), regulatory agencies (International Organisation of Securities Commissions, IOSCO; the Securities and Exchange Commission, SEC) and Credit Rating Agencies (including Standard and Poors, Moodys and Fitch). These reports have all recommended that Boards of Directors identify and monitor company risks, including financial risks, and report on these risks to investors.

This monograph examines one risk in particular: IRR. Bartram (2002) states that IRR is as volatile as foreign exchange (FX) rate risk, but that it is rarely studied. He notes that this topic is important as interest rate movements are related to changes in the business cycle, with a time lag, with an effect on the cost of capital of companies, which in turn influences the investment behaviour and competitive positioning of firms; all these factors have implications for the future cash flows of firms, and hence, their market value.

This chapter reviews the relevant prior literature and covers a variety of different aspects of corporate risk management. Specifically, the review begins with an examination of the definition of risk and then analyses the three types of risk behaviour in finance: arbitrage, hedging and speculation. Next, it explores the rationale for the corporate management of financial risk, and then introduces readers to the two particular forms of financial risk, IRR and FX rate risk. The chapter then examines IRR in detail followed by a review of the prior empirical research into the use of derivatives to manage financial risk in general, and IRR specifically. Finally, the last two sub-sections look into the corporate governance aspects of derivative monitoring and control, and the derivative disclosure regulations with reference to the Cadbury and Turnbull Reports and the financial instrument accounting standards FRS 13, IAS 39 and FAS 133, respectively. Following the widespread development of financial derivatives, the 1990s witnessed a number of different financial scandals involving the use of financial derivatives. As a consequence, regulators, including the International Accounting Standards Board (IASB) sought to develop rules to prevent any future inappropriate practices.

2.2 Risk and uncertainty

The word 'risk' may conjure up many different ideas in people's minds depending upon their background, expertise, or position in society. To an engineer, risk may relate to the possibility of a bridge collapsing or a building falling down and the subsequent consequences of such an occurrence. To an environmentalist, the focus on risk may be the well-being of the planet. An insurer or an actuarist may be concerned with the financial consequences of the risk that some catastrophe will occur or that people will live longer than expected. As Burgess (2003) notes 'Risk is a fundamental of existence – a balancing of one thing against another, neither of which may be known' (p. 32).

Business executives in organisations throughout the world have many risks to consider, but many of these focus upon a subset of their organisation's risks depending upon their functional specialism (Helliar *et al.*, 2001). This monograph investigates one particular risk, that of IRR, and examines the management of this risk by UK companies, especially from the viewpoint of those functionally responsible for it: UK corporate treasurers.

In the context of this monograph, the word 'risk' is a generic one that encompasses both risk and uncertainty. In the neo-classical economic literature there is a clear difference between risk and uncertainty. The word risk is derived from the early Italian word *risicare* that means 'to dare' (Bernstein, 1996). In their classic work on organisations, March and Simon (1958) defined the term 'risk' to include those situations where decision-makers knew the probability distribution of the consequences of each alternative outcome that might occur. The situation where all possible consequences are known, but where it is not possible to assign definite probabilities to particular outcomes, has been referred to as 'uncertainty' (Knight, 1921). However, the perception of the word 'risk' and 'uncertainty' has moved on since Knight and March and Simon conducted their seminal works, and as Burgess (2003) indicates, most situations that are risky are also uncertain: 'If you can reduce things to monetary criteria then either the question was trivial or you probably haven't understood it.'

Overall, consistent with many current texts, this monograph treats the two terms, risk and uncertainty, as synonymous.

2.3 Defining arbitrage, hedging and speculation

There are three main types of risk activities undertaken by participants in the financial markets: arbitrage, hedging and speculation (Galitz, 1994). Arbitrage enables a risk-free profit to be made by taking advantage of: (i) price discrepancies from geographical and time differences in two or more markets; or (ii) price variations in different product markets at the same point in time, such as between the cash market and the futures market. Hedging is where a financial risk is eliminated or reduced by passing the risk on to someone else and this is the activity that is usually used by corporate treasurers in managing their IRR. Finally, speculation occurs when a view is taken about the likely direction of prices or rates in the market; the speculator hopes to make a profit if the price moves in the predicted direction. A classic example of this form of activity would be someone buying shares and hoping that the price of these shares will rise.

The difference between hedging and speculation, is, however, not always distinguishable. Some researchers (and managers alike) believe that a decision to leave an exposure open and not hedge it, is a form of speculation. Others regard such a decision to fall within their scope of hedging activity. As Ankrom (1974) suggested:

> It is important that the distinction between an un-hedged and a speculative position be explicitly recognised in order to avoid costly policy mistakes which would call for total hedging all the time. (p. 88)

The Bank of England Quarterly Bulletin (1995) also highlights the grey area between hedging and speculation/trading. It argues that in situations when companies use non-conventional approaches to manage their financial risks:

> The main difficulty here is to distinguish trading from [this] dynamic hedging, because the latter may involve frequent adjustment of derivative positions to maintain a hedged book. Sophisticated treasury operations hedge on a portfolio basis rather than transaction by transaction so, as a firm's underlying cash portfolio changes and its management's view of likely market or economic developments evolves, existing hedges may be closed out or offset and new hedges put on. Such dynamic hedging may be difficult to distinguish objectively – either in scale or in pattern – from trading. (p. 186)

Thus, dynamic hedges enacted by management to manage their financial risks may be misconstrued as speculative activity by outsiders.

The level of hedging that managers undertake depends upon their attitude to risk. In their study of FX risk management, Belk and Glaum (1990) found that managers in nine of the sixteen companies they visited were initially classified as risk averse and only three managers appeared to be risk-seeking. However, on further investigation, staff in only three of the companies that they visited appeared to be truly risk averse. They concluded that:

> Only a minority were risk averse in the full meaning of the term. The majority to varying degrees accepted the risks inherent in uncovered foreign exchange exposures, or even sought to increase these risks in order to profit from their foreign exchange risk management. (p. 11)

A practitioner in Belk and Glaum's (1990) study further clarified hedging into active and passive hedging. He stated:

> Consider a treasury that is seeking to manage a naturally long USD exposure. Electing to simply sell surplus USD each time these are identified would be 'passive hedging'. A treasury that has the flexibility to both sell and buy USD when considered appropriate is displaying an 'active hedging' management approach. If that treasury were permitted to create contracts and unrelated exposures by dealing in JPY, for example, that would clearly be speculation.

He also notes that other ways to manage risk are to avoid, prevent, control or mitigate and that for residual risk, the choice is whether to retain or transfer it through hedging.

However, in general, prior researchers have found that companies actively managed their exposures. Thus, the first two research questions addressed in this study are whether: (i) IRR is important to UK firms, irrespective of size; and (ii) whether UK companies actively manage their interest rate exposure.

2.4 The rationale for corporate risk management and hedging

Mian (1996) defines hedging as 'the activities undertaken by the firm in order to mitigate the impact of . . . uncertainties on the value of the firm' (p. 419). This definition is the same basis as Froot, Scharfstein and Stein's (1994) analysis of the topic. They illustrate the main benefits of hedging by drawing on the story of the Pharaoh and Joseph: during the seven years of plenty, people stored food and grain and when the seven years of famine arrived, they used these reserves and had enough food to survive the famine. Hedging can, therefore, be viewed as a continuous response by risk-averse individuals to the uncertain economic future that their companies face.

However, the early finance literature argued that companies did not need to manage their risks or hedge their exposures. For example, Modigliani and Miller (1958) argued that whatever a company could do, investors could replicate. Therefore, if a company was exposed to exchange rate or IRR, this exposure did not need to be hedged by the company since investors could do this for themselves. In addition, the Capital Asset Pricing Model

(CAPM) suggests that firms should not hedge their exposures. According to the CAPM, only systematic risk is important; any risk that is unsystematic can be diversified away by investors in the process of portfolio construction. However, according to CAPM, even if an exposure is systematic, corporate hedging should not be necessary. That is, if hedging instruments are priced according to the CAPM, a firm that hedges will simply move along the security market line; there will be no increase in firm value.

Further, Holland (1993) argued that, over the long term, hedging might not be necessary if the expected value of the gains and losses over time were calculated to be zero. However, it would be little consolation if the timing of a large foreign currency receivable coincided with a large negative change in the exchange rate to know that it would correct itself with an equivalent gain in the long run. If the markets were efficient, there would be no need to hedge, but companies might need to consider capital market imperfections such as tax regimes, unexpected changes in interest rates, inflation rates and exchange rates as well as changes in their own operations.

However, in reality, risk management is widely used by finance directors, corporate treasurers and portfolio managers to reduce the volatility of their firm's reported profit. Several reasons have been advanced in the literature to explain why companies hedge their exposure. First, Smith and Stulz (1985) argued that hedging reduces the expected costs of bankruptcy because it lowered the likelihood of financial distress by reducing the variance of firm value. They further argued that because the probability of a firm experiencing financial distress was directly related to the size of the firm's fixed claims relative to the value of its assets, hedging would become more valuable as the fixed claims of a firm rose.

Second, it has been argued that firm's hedge to minimise the variability in cash flows, thereby increasing firm value. In particular, Froot, Scharfstein and Stein (1993) reason that if a firm does not hedge, there will be some variability in cash flows that will disturb the investment and financing plans in a way that is costly to the firm. The third reason that has been advanced in the literature to explain why companies hedge their exposures focuses on capital market imperfections and inefficient investment. This explanation rests on the observation that if firms choose not to hedge their exposures, they may be forced to underinvest because of the expense of, or inability to raise, external finance.

Fourth, Stulz (1984) argues that firms may engage in hedging to protect managerial self-interest. While the central tenets of the CAPM imply that corporate hedging is unnecessary because of the ability of investors to diversify, this argument may not hold for managers who may have a relatively large portion of their wealth invested in the firm. Thus, managers may be motivated to undertake corporate hedging in order to reduce the variance of total firm value, thereby improving their own risk/return trade-off. Finally, some commentators have argued that hedging can lower tax payments for a company facing a progressive corporate tax schedule (Mayers and Smith, 1982; Smith and Stulz, 1985; Rawls and Smithson, 1990). This result arises from the convexity of the corporate tax structure (caused by progressive taxes and tax shields) and the fact that hedging reduces the variance of the firm's taxable income. In particular, in the presence of a convex tax code, hedging can be beneficial if it ensures that taxable income falls within the optimal range of tax rates. That is, risk management can lead to lower tax payments. These capital market imperfections of the neo-classical model of economic theory are now widely accepted, and it is recognised that companies employ specialised staff to conduct hedging operations (Helliar, 1997). This monograph accepts these postulates and assumes that corporate financial risk management is an important technique that is used by a wide variety of companies.

2.5 Interest rate and foreign exchange risk management

Companies often face two key financial risk exposures; IRR and FX rate risk (Holland, 1993; Brigham and Gapenski, 1994; Buckley, 2000). IRR is concerned with the variability of profit, cash flows or the valuation of a company to movements in interest rates (Buckley, 2000). FX exposure arises because currency movements may affect the home currency values and potentially affect the firm's competitiveness (Buckley, 2000). Buckley (2000) argues that FX exposure can be categorised into three different types of exposure: translation exposure, transaction exposure and economic exposure. Translation exposure reflects the gain or loss arising from the consolidation of financial statements, while transaction exposure arises from the settlement of a future payment or receipt denominated in a foreign currency, the amount of which will fluctuate due to changes in exchange rates. Finally, economic exposure relates to future corporate strategy, where the objective is to enhance competitiveness by maximising economic value over the long term (Belk and Glaum, 1990; Moffet and Karlsen, 1994). FX risk can be managed through the use of both internal and external hedging techniques. Internal hedging techniques are intended to reduce exposed positions, or prevent them from arising, and consist of techniques such as netting, matching, leading and lagging, pricing policies and asset/liability management (Buckley, 2000). By contrast, external hedging techniques can be undertaken through an intermediary, such as a bank or a dealer, and involve the use of derivatives including forwards, futures, options and swaps.

A review of the literature indicates that many studies have examined FX rate risk management, but there appears to be a dearth of work in the IRR management area (Bartram, 2002). A third research question that will, therefore, be examined in this study is whether IRR management or FX risk management is considered more important to the financial positions of UK companies.

2.6 Interest rate risk

Interest rate risk is probably the most important of all the financial risks which organisations may face as there are several ways in which changes in interest rates can affect a business (Phillips, 1995). First, a company may have debt or bank overdraft finance linked to market interest rates such as the bank base rate or LIBOR[2], and as interest rates change, the interest payable on these borrowings may also vary. A highly geared company, with a large amount of debt financing relative to equity capital, may suffer financial distress if interest rates increase dramatically. Second, a decrease in

[2]London Interbank Offered Rate.

interest rates will reduce the interest income for an organisation that has surplus cash invested in monetary deposits and floating-rate investments. Third, an increase in interest rates may adversely affect an organisation's business if its customers are reluctant to make purchases when interest rates are high because they have less disposable income available; this scenario is especially true for the UK where a high percentage of the population have mortgages with repayments linked to current interest rates. Fourth, suppliers may raise their prices to cover the increase in their funding costs. This price increase may have a detrimental effect on the financial performance of the supplied business. In some businesses it may be possible to pass on raw material price increases to customers, but in other organisations, where competition is fierce or the industry is regulated, this option may not be available. For example, in a recession, a supermarket may be able to pass on price increases but a utility with a regulated pricing policy, or a manufacturer of luxury goods, may not be able to do so. In the worst case scenario, high interest rates may increase both input costs and interest payments on finance, as well as encourage customers to postpone their purchases. Some organisations will be more exposed to the negative effects of high interest rates than others. Highly geared manufacturers of luxury goods are likely to be more sensitive to interest rate rises than lowly geared supermarkets; the former will thus have far more to gain from managing their IRR effectively.

The last few decades have seen an increase in the globalisation of the world's financial markets, and this may have affected the nature of IRR management within companies. For example, Titman (2002) argues that practitioners often talk 'about window of opportunity', and 'market conditions' when deciding upon fund raising and related hedging and cost reduction strategies. For example, the spread between a credit rating of AAA and that of BBB has averaged about 120 basis points, but this spread changes substantially, both narrowing and widening at certain times in the economic cycle. Further, he argues that the corporate bond default spread has often been too wide relative to the observed risk premia in the equity markets. Thus, companies may be paying more for each unit of risk when raising debt finance, with resulting IRR management consequences. Titman (2002) also observes that companies are likely to borrow in the shorter-term markets when the term structure of interest rates is steep, but to borrow in the long-term debt markets when the yield curve is flatter. Hence it can be argued that treasurers may adopt IRR management techniques to reduce their cost of capital by timing the debt markets.

Similarly, Ross (2002) describes treasurers' decisions on the fixed and floating-rate debt mix, and advises on a two-stage methodology to deal with IRR exposure. First, he suggests that an appropriate level of gearing is adopted, and second, for that level of gearing, an appropriate amount of fixed-rate debt is selected. The maturity of the debt profile and gearing will be influenced by the desired credit rating and the stability of the businesses' cash flows. Where cash flows are volatile, a lower level of gearing is more appropriate. The more difficult decision, according to Ross, is the amount of debt to hedge, by fixing the interest payments and the maturity of this debt. This decision is affected by: (i) how the business responds to economic cycles; (ii) the effect that interest rate changes have on the company; (iii) the existence of banking covenants; and (iv) the competitive position of the organisation. Companies that can change their prices as inflation rates rise can have mainly floating-rate debt financing. He argues that interest rates follow the yield curve, that the yield curve is normally positive and thus it costs more to borrow longer at fixed rates (although the UK has had a history of negative yield curves so this may not necessarily apply to the UK!).

In contrast, companies that cannot easily change their selling prices, have long-term contracts or fixed income flows, should lock in a margin by fixing their interest cost. He cites the building and construction industry as a prime example of an industry where companies would probably wish to have fixed-rate debt in their capital structure. On the subject of covenants, Ross advises that companies need to manage their debt to earnings before interest, tax, depreciation and amortisation (EBITDA) or their EBITDA to their interest expense. Mortimer (2003) agrees and states that volatility should be measured according to LIBOR rates and the correlation of the EBITDA to LIBOR. He further notes that 'the volatility of interest rate payments can affect the credit rating and covenant interest coverage ratios' (p. 47).

Douche (2002) suggests that in conditions of volatile rates of interest and inflation, companies should borrow floating-rate finance if they expect rates to fall further than the yield curve suggests, or borrow fixed-rate finance otherwise, and use options if they are uncertain. Douche also states that building and construction companies should hold fixed-rate finance as demand for their products normally goes down as interest rates go up. However, he suggests that retail organisations should buy caps to put a ceiling on the amount of interest that they may have to pay, as the retail industry is very competitive, and the cost of borrowing is often a crucial component of their profitability. However, as caps are costly derivative products, he recommends that retailers should use floating-rate finance and only use caps when they really believe interest rates will rise. For the more general business, he recommends that treasurers take a view and, if they think that rates are going down, they assume the maximum amount of floating-rate finance as possible, but if they expect rates to increase, they should have the highest amount possible of fixed-rate finance. Thus, Douche expects treasurers to take an active view on the movement of interest rates and to base their hedging decisions upon these views. However, he notes that Boards of Directors need to have confidence in their treasurers and most Boards set bands within which treasurers may manoeuvre, often on a currency by currency basis.

2.7 Derivatives usage: Evidence from prior empirical research

One of the main activities of the treasury department in an organisation is the management of IRR. There are several ways in which this task can be accomplished, though one of the most common ways is to use derivative products, including interest rate swaps, forward rate agreements (FRAs), interest rate futures and options.

As Crockett (1996) states:

> The fundamental contribution of derivative instruments lies in their power to target risk; to break complex risks down into their constituent elements and allow them to be separately priced and traded. This enables much more effective risk management. (p. 18)

The remainder of this section reviews the results of prior empirical research into corporate derivative activity. First, it summarises studies from around the globe and then examines in further detail a selection of these studies.

Several studies have surveyed derivatives usage in western countries such as in Belgium, Germany, New Zealand, the UK and the US. These surveys have found that, for FX risk management, forwards are the most commonly used instruments, followed by OTC options and swaps. For IRR management, interest rate swaps have dominated corporate practice, followed by OTC options and forwards (Bodnar, Hayt and Marston, 1996; Bodnar and Gebhardt, 1998; Prevost, Rose and Miller, 2000). In general, most surveys have found that companies use derivatives to manage their cash flows and fluctuations in accounting earnings (Bodnar *et al.*, 1995; Bodnar and Gebhardt, 1998; Prevost, Rose and Miller, 2000).

Studies of non-financial firms in New Zealand and the US have shown that derivatives usage is often related to company size, with larger firms using more derivatives. Possible explanations may be that: (i) the risk exposures of smaller firms are too small relative to standard contract sizes; and (ii) larger firms may have a greater range of exposures for which derivatives may be needed (Bodnar *et al.*, 1995; Prevost, Rose and Miller, 2000). However, other studies, such as in Germany and the US, have found that derivatives usage is consistent over all size groups (Bodnar and Gebhardt, 1998). By examining the IRR management practices of both large and small companies, this project extends the literature on the general use of derivatives by examining whether larger companies manage their financial risk to a greater extent than smaller companies.

Academics at the Wharton Business School published two questionnaire-based articles about the hedging policies adopted and usage of derivatives by US firms (Bodnar *et al.*, 1995; Bodnar, Hayt and Marston, 1996). These studies covered a wider range of derivative products than the earlier study of Block and Gallagher (1986), and reported that about 40 per cent of those companies that were surveyed used risk management instruments such as forwards, options and swaps. However, the later studies found that a higher proportion of larger companies used these instruments. In particular, companies from all industrial sectors used swaps, although service sector firms used them less than other sectors such as manufacturing. Three quarters of those that used derivatives hedged FX risk. In this respect, the most popular instruments used were FX forwards, followed by OTC options.

About three quarters of the respondents also hedged IRR, and interest rate swaps were the most popular product employed for this purpose. The four main goals of hedging were found to be: (i) to manage the volatility of accounting earnings; (ii) to reduce cashflow variability; (iii) to manage the balance sheet; and (iv) to maximise the market value of the company. Hedging was most common for contractual commitments and least important for translating the balance sheet and managing economic exposure. The majority of firms hedged short-term commitments with short-term instruments. Three quarters of companies had documented policies regarding the use of derivatives but just over half had no regular schedule of reporting hedging activities to the Board of Directors.

At the same time as the Wharton Business School were investigating this topic, a comprehensive survey into the use of derivatives by US firms was conducted by Phillips (1995). On 30 December 1994, a sample of members of the Treasury Management Association were surveyed. Phillips found that 63 per cent of companies used derivatives for either managing risk, obtaining funding or investing. This survey was broader than that of the Wharton school; Phillips focused on derivative securities as well as derivative instruments and, for instance, included bond issues with derivative features. He documented that 90 per cent of respondents thought that they were exposed to IRR, 75 per cent believed they faced FX rate risk and 37 per cent said that they were exposed to commodity price risk. Risk management was the most important use of derivative instruments, while the role of these products in raising finance for investment purposes was cited by only a small minority of the respondents. OTC instruments were preferred by a majority of executives surveyed mainly because of the flexibility they offered in matching exposure. For instance, respondents preferred using OTC rather than exchange-traded options. Phillips found that interest rate swaps were the preferred instrument for hedging IRR while FX forwards were the most popular for hedging FX rate risk.

Other researchers have examined published financial statements rather than using survey questionnaire responses. For example, Hentschel and Kothari (1995) analysed the financial statements of 425 US companies and found that a small number of firms accounted for a large part of the derivatives activity. Just over one-half of non-financial organisations disclosed details on their use of derivatives. They found that these companies generally used more FX derivatives, especially FX forwards, and held about twice as many forwards as swaps. Those companies that used derivatives had a notional principal value of derivatives of about 14 per cent of total assets.

Studies have also been carried out into the use of derivatives by non-US companies (see for example Berkman and Bradbury (1996) and Berkman *et al.* (1997b)). Berkman and Bradbury (1996) studied the financial accounts of the 116 companies listed on the New Zealand Stock Exchange that had to report the fair value and notional value of all their off- and on-balance sheet financial instruments. They examined three rationales for hedging: (i) managerial risk aversion; (ii) the minimisation of risks associated with the level of foreign activity; and (iii) the need to co-ordinate finance and investment policies. They found that derivatives usage increased with certain financial characteristics such as leverage, size, the existence of tax losses, the proportion of shares held by directors and the dividend payout ratio. The use of derivatives was lower for firms with high interest coverage and high liquidity. They also discovered that short-term asset growth, the proportion of foreign assets and the use of alternative capital market instruments were not related to derivative usage. They argued that a company had more flexibility in adjusting the size, maturity and denomination of its financial instruments than in adjusting its operating and financing strategies and thus derivatives might be used by firms that experienced difficulties in varying their operating activities in response to changes in economic variables. They also found support for the views that: (i) hedging was used to exploit economies of scale associated with transaction costs; and (ii) larger companies with more sophisticated financial management were more likely to employ hedging techniques. Companies using derivatives tended to be more highly geared and have higher dividend payout ratios than their non-user counterparts. The authors fitted a Tobit model to their data and concluded that firms used derivatives to reduce the cost of financial distress and increase the present value of tax losses. They also suggested that a low dividend payout ratio and a high proportion of liquid assets reduced the need to use derivative instruments when attempting to lower agency costs. Companies that hedged tended to have a greater proportion of shares held by Directors. Executives might, therefore, have used these products to reduce the variability of their firm's value by maintaining earnings and dividend payouts.

A more recent study conducted by Dunne *et al.* (2003) found that company size and the extent to which a company's turnover came from overseas were the two most significant factors in explaining the disclosure about derivatives usage. This finding supports the theory that companies that hedge do so for reasons of economies of scale and the existence of hedging alternatives.

2.8 Interest rate risk management

As noted above, empirical studies investigating the management of IRR are fairly limited. While Grant and Marshall (1997) and Helliar (1997) looked into the corporate usage of interest rate derivatives and interest rate swaps, respectively, there is little in the literature in terms of the operations of the entire IRR management function in the UK. Few studies have been carried out elsewhere, with the exception of Block and Gallagher (1986) and Dolde (1993) who examined corporate practices in the US, and Batten, Mellor and Wan (1994) and Hakkarainen, Kasanen and Puttonen (1997) who focused on Australian and Finnish firms, respectively.

Motivated by the fact that the swaps market had seen the largest growth of any financial market in the world during the 1980s and 1990s, Helliar (1997) investigated the use of interest rate and currency swaps by UK firms. The volume of swaps traded in the world today is now in the trillions (thousands of billions) of dollars per annum and in the hundreds of billions on a daily basis (Freidman and Joseph, 1993; Bank of England Quarterly Bulletin, 2001). The main reason for the increase in the interest rate derivatives market has been the rise in interest rate swaps of 106 per cent in the three-year period since 1998, especially the Euro-Overnight Index Average Swaps contract (EONIA). The use of FRAs rose by 96 per cent, although interest rate options contracts saw a rise of only 10 per cent, which reduced their overall share of the market to merely 5 per cent. In 2001, \$83 billion of FRAs, \$142 billion of swaps and \$13 billion of options were traded daily. Most trading of interest rate derivatives occurred in London, and 132 financial institutions traded there, as opposed to only 77 institutions that traded currency derivatives (Bank of England Quarterly Bulletin, 2001).

The Block and Gallagher (1986) study concentrated exclusively on the use of interest rate futures and options. The authors examined the reasons for the use (or lack of use) of these instruments, the organisational authority that was required to transact in these products and whether firms employed analytical techniques to appraise their effectiveness. The authors found that while there were some users of futures and options, the most common reason for non-use was the objections from top-level management, who often were not sufficiently knowledgeable about these products to sanction their use.

As part of his survey into the management of corporate financial risk, Dolde (1993) examined the management of IRR together with that of exchange rate risk. In particular, Dolde (1993) looked into the organisational issues surrounding the management process, the personnel involved and the level of centralisation of the risk management function; the objectives guiding the risk management process and the level of integration of the function into the firm's overall financial and strategic plans were examined. The author concluded that corporate strategies were gaining momentum with financial managers and that a better understanding and assessment of their exposures was extending their use of financial instruments, and also prioritising their risk management objectives. However, it was noticeable that the management of IRR received less attention than the management of FX rate risk.

In an Australian context, Batten, Mellor and Wan (1994) examined the IRR management practices of firms by analysing the type of funding that was raised and the financial instruments that were used by the sampled firms, both in domestic and international markets. The authors also explored how companies measured and managed their IRR, and the use of technology and banking contacts in the risk management process. Their results suggested that the management of IRR factored highly in respondent firms, where a variety of numerical techniques were used to measure IRR and a range of derivative products were used to manage this risk.

In a European setting, similar findings to those of the US and Australia have been documented. The corporate practices of the largest 100 Finnish firms were reviewed by Hakkarainen, Kasanen and Puttonen (1997) who examined: (i) the attitudes and policies guiding the risk management process; (ii) the methods used to assess the level of risk, including the use of interest rate forecasts; (iii) the use of hedging instruments; and (iv) the success of risk management strategies in Finnish firms. The study found that most firms attempted to manage their IRR, although the use of technical risk measures and sophisticated financial instruments were restricted to the larger firms. However, there was no significant association between the degree of leverage and the use of hedging instruments.

A direct comparison of the above studies is difficult not only because they cover different time frames, but also because the focus and research methodologies of the studies differ. For example, while Block and Gallagher (1986) focused principally on the use of IRR management instruments, the more recent study by Hakkarainen, Kasanen and Puttonen (1997) also examined risk measurement techniques, use of interest rate forecasts and the success of corporate management strategies. Nonetheless, some synthesis can be gained from these prior studies to inform the current research. Four further aims of this research are, therefore, to investigate: (i) the funding, equity and gearing levels that are common; (ii) whether the same factors pertain in all firms; (iii) the forecasting methods used by UK companies; and (iv) whether derivative products are used, and whether particular derivative products, such as interest rate swaps, are preferred to others in certain circumstances.

2.9 Corporate governance and the disclosure of risk

The above analysis has demonstrated that companies around the world face risks on a daily basis and that companies often employ different strategies for managing these risks, especially financial risks associated with interest rate movements. However, another aspect of risk is corporate governance and the disclosure of, and accountability for, risk identification, evaluation and management, to corporate stakeholders.

As early as 1992, the Cadbury report set out recommendations relating to the identification, evaluation and management of business risks and also encouraged enterprises to disclose specific key risks. Indeed, the UK Stock Exchange's requirements are very clear about the publication of information on financial risks that might be material for stakeholder's decisions. The London Stock Exchange's Listing Rules require companies to disclose 'all special trade factors or risks'. The ICAEW December 1997 Risk Report recommended that:

> [L]isted companies should present an operating review, including a discussion identifying the principal risks and uncertainties in the main lines of business, together with a commentary on the approach to managing these risks and, in qualitative terms, the nature of the potential impact on results. (Section 3.9)

In addition, all quoted firms on the major US Stock Exchanges must make disclosures about their concentration of risk, both general and specific, to the enterprise under the American Institute of Certified Public Accountants (AICPA) Statement of Practice 94–6. In the UK, senior managers should undertake a risk review, the nature and scope of which is outlined in the Turnbull report:

> The [directors'] review should cover all controls, including financial, operational and compliance controls and risk management (p. 3) . . . and will depend upon . . . the scale, diversity and complexity of the company's operations; and the nature of the significant risks that the company faces (p. 8) . . . and should consider what are the significant risks and assess how they have been identified, evaluated and managed. (p. 9)

This greater control and monitoring of risks at a senior level might reduce the cost of capital for a firm, encourage the adoption of better risk management techniques and practices and improve the accountability of senior managers to shareholders and other stakeholder groups. These recommendations on risk management and risk reporting arose from various corporate governance codes that were issued during the 1990s, where the central tenet was an emphasis on internal control. The recent Risk Management Survey by the ICAEW (2002) found that financial and strategic risks were the two risks most engaged in by the Board of Directors. As part of this process, adequate reporting structures were required to ensure the sufficient control of treasury and the risk management functions (Linsley and Shrives, 2001). Raeburn and Gunson (2003) note that the most effective and value-enhancing financial risk management activities can be undermined by a poor governance and control framework.

The reports identified above were responses to scandals and concerns that preceded their publication. Consequently, the corporate governance practices of major companies have received widespread attention in recent years, particularly the monitoring and control of publicly held corporations. These concerns have grown markedly in the last year in the wake of difficulties at high profile organisations such as Enron, whose demise was due in part to the use of Special Purpose Vehicles to hide the use of energy derivatives (Bensten and Hartgraves, 2002; Revsine, 1991).

Further, the past few decades have shown that, even pre-Enron, derivatives such as swaps, options and futures have attracted much negative publicity. Taking interest rate swaps as an example, the most notorious case in the UK was the local councils' swaps fiasco (Accountancy Age, 1992; Gastineau, 1993), notably the Hammersmith and Fulham court case, where the court ruled that the swaps transactions that Hammersmith and Fulham had entered into were *ultra vires* and that any payments on such contracts were null and void. At the time, local authorities were paying large sums of money to the banks through these contracts and it is estimated that the banks lost hundreds of millions of pounds as a result of this judgement. More recent cases have involved legal actions about leveraged swaps in the US, such as Gibsons Greetings and Proctor and Gamble[3], where the companies claimed that the banks that sold them the products did not inform them of all the consequences of undertaking these swap contracts (Business Week, 1994; Overdahl and Schachter, 1995; Chew, 1996). More recently, both the Baring's crisis and Allied Irish Bank's US subsidiary All First Financial have cast their shadow over the control and monitoring of individuals that use derivative products (Leeson, 1996; Dunne and Helliar, 2002; Raeburn and Gunson, 2003). Indeed, Mansell (2003) argues that many of these failings

[3]Leveraged swaps are where a company in certain circumstances may take on an increased exposure to interest rates.

lie at Board of Director level, where typically the Board lack treasury and finance skills, does not prioritise treasury highly enough and has a preconceived view of treasury activities. Hogan (1997) also claimed that Barings' collapse had to do with 'the failure of management in its monitoring and analysis of trading activities and the risk associated with them' (p. 14). Similarly, the failings at Orange County were also due to the failings of management in adequately supervising the activities of its staff (Jorion, 1995).

Such failings in corporate governance can have an adverse impact on treasury operations, as a company with poor corporate governance may find it harder to access funds and may also find that funding costs increase, credit-rating downgrades become more common and investor confidence weakens. The mechanisms of corporate governance are seen as integral tenets in the operation of modern corporations; 'good' corporate governance is seen as essential in terms of safeguarding company assets, and maintaining and enhancing investor confidence and, thus, providing greater access to funds and reducing the potential risks associated with fraud. However, despite the bad publicity that these cases have attracted, treasurers continue to increase their usage of these financial instruments. Thus, the eighth research question that is addressed in this monograph seeks to understand why these products are used, the policies and practices surrounding their use and the effectiveness of corporate governance.

2.10 Accounting for financial instruments

The analysis above suggests that greater disclosure can assist in the corporate governance and internal control mechanisms of organisations. McDonough (1993) noted that the increased use of derivatives and inadequacy of accounting requirements reduced the transparency of company exposures. A year later, in 1994, the Jenkins Report echoed a similar concern about the lack of disclosure in financial statements to assist investors in understanding the effects of their derivatives transactions. To meet this need for more information, the ASB introduced FRS 13 in 1998. This Standard became effective for accounting periods ending on or after 23 March 1999. The Standard requires entities with publicly traded capital instruments, and all financial institutions other than insurance companies, to give sufficient narrative and numerical disclosures regarding their use of derivatives and other financial instruments. The main purpose of the narrative disclosures is to stimulate a discussion of the company's objectives for using financial instruments and the role that these instruments have played in the overall risk management strategy of the company (ASB, 1998). The aim of the numerical disclosures is to show how the policies are implemented and to provide supplementary information for evaluating the magnitude of any significant exposures (ASB, 1998). The standard has a number of sections that should be addressed in the Annual Report including: objectives, policies and strategies, IRR, currency risk, liquidity risk, fair values, hedge accounting, commodity contracts, market price risk, accounting policies and 'general other'.

However, a number of commentators have criticised certain aspects of FRS 13. For example, the standard has been labelled as 'unclear' by several critics (Bircher, 1999), while the Financial Reporting Review Panel (FRRP) has issued a general warning, stating that it has already had to take a number of companies to task about their failure to abide by the guidelines (Hinks, 2001). Companies that have incurred the wrath of the FRRP include Artisan, Ensor Holdings and Wiggins; indeed in 2002 the latter was forced by the panel to restate its accounts from 1996 to 2000 (Hinks, 2001).

Adedeji and Baker (1999) uncovered a large gap between the requirements of FRS 13 and the reporting practice that existed prior to the introduction of the standard. In a survey carried out by PricewaterhouseCoopers, McIlwraith and Dealy (2000) conducted a review of FRS 13's implementation based on the disclosures made by sixty companies from the FTSE 500. They found that of the sixty firms whose financial statements were reviewed, ten were 'early adopters', having year-ends on or before the Standard became mandatory in March 1999, while the other fifty were obliged to comply. The authors found that the explanations put forward concerning the use of derivatives, and the policies in place, seemed 'incomplete'. However, Dunne *et al.* (2003) found from their content analysis of annual reports that derivative disclosure had doubled since the release of the standard. In addition, in interviews with both preparers and users of financial statements, the authors found that narrative disclosures were welcomed.

Both UK and international organisations support the disclosure of risk-related information to groups that are interested in the current performance and long-run survival of an enterprise. However, the risks that are highlighted are often described in only very general terms and vary from one report to another. The introduction of FRS 13 in the UK, Financial Accounting Standard (FAS) 133 and 138 in the US and IAS 39 internationally, have all helped to inform stakeholders of the financial risks that companies undertake, including that of IRR.

Overall, despite the negative reactions and criticisms towards FRS 13, there have been positive attributes to the standard and its implementation has been a fairly painless process as most of the requirements were in the form of notes and disclosures to the accounts (Helliar, Dunne and Moir, 2004). In January 2005, however, FRS 13 was superseded by IAS 39 – Financial Instruments: Recognition and Measurement – following the introduction of the international accounting standards to the European Commission (Awty, 2001).

International Accounting Standard 39, introduced for financial statements starting on the 1 January 2001 or thereafter, is based on the earlier US standard FAS 133: Accounting for Derivative Instruments and Hedging Activities. Issued in June 1998[4,5], the goal of FAS 133 (and in turn, IAS 39), like FRS 13, is to provide investors with more information on companies' risk management practices and derivative transactions. However, FAS 133 goes further than FRS 13 by requiring that financial statements not only provide notes and disclosures, but also that the impact of any hedging activity must be reflected through the earnings statement. In particular, FAS 133 requires that an entity: (i) recognises all derivatives as either assets or liabilities in the statement of financial position; (ii) measures these instruments at fair value; and (iii) incorporates any changes in fair values into the profit and loss account.

---

[4]'FAS 137 Accounting for Derivative Instruments and Hedging Activities—Deferral of the Effective Date of FASB Statement No. 133—An Amendment of FASB Statement No. 133' was issued in June 1999 deferring the adoption date for FAS 133 to January 2001.

[5]'FAS 138 Accounting for Certain Derivative Instruments and Certain Hedging Activities—An Amendment of FASB Statement No. 133' was issued in June 2000.

Osterland (2001) cited an Association for Finance Professionals (AFP) survey that found that more than two-thirds of the respondents thought that FAS 133 had imposed an excessive burden on reporting companies. He noted that most of the frustration with FAS 133 stemmed from the issue of hedge accounting. The requirements of FAS 133 for organisations to document every hedge from the outset and to mark-to-market their derivatives every quarter were proving quite difficult even for larger companies, with General Electric reported to have spent $8 million over a two-year period developing systems to perform these functions (Osterland, 2001). Further, although interest rate swaps and currency forwards have been the preferred derivative products of treasurers, this choice has been further enhanced at the expense of interest rate and currency options. Overall, FAS 133 appears to have changed treasurers' operational practices.

Di Paola and Cattoor (2000) indicated that FAS 133 was sure to drive changes in treasury policy. However, they noted that despite these changes, many companies were beginning to see the positive side to FAS 133. They indicated that some companies viewed the standard as an opportunity to get treasury 'out of its ivory tower' and closer to the central business function. The authors also suggested that the implementation of the standard allowed companies to ensure that exposures were properly captured and that hedging policies were aligned to corporate objectives.

The expected introduction of IAS 39 in UK companies appears to have caused preparers a great deal of concern (Foulkes, 2002). Together with posing as a regulatory system that will result in high set-up costs, the fair-value accounting treatment of financial instruments, and the subsequent requirements to report any change in these values through the profit and loss account, may create large variations in earnings figures (Helliar *et al.*, 2002b). Management may, as a result, curtail their current activity and stop using some of these products altogether. This is especially so if some of the recommendations of the Joint Working Group (JWG), as discussed below, set up by the International Accounting Standards Committee (IASC) are taken on board by the IASB.

Before the issuance of IAS 39, the IASC set up the JWG in November 1997 to explore the possibility of full fair-value accounting for all financial assets and liabilities. Comprising thirteen national accounting standard setters, the JWG was disbanded on the formation of the IASB. Its findings, as reported in December 2000 were, however, adopted for discussion by the IASB. Like FAS 133 and IAS 39, the report by the JWG also supported the notion of fair-value accounting and the need to report any changes in value in the profit and loss account. It was however, more stringent than the two accounting standards in at least one core respect: it prohibited the use of hedge accounting, an accounting treatment that the IAS 39 and the FAS 133 allow. The next sub-section discusses in detail the principles of hedge accounting and the views of the JWG.

2.11 Hedge accounting

The central difference between the JWG and the FAS 133 and IAS 39 approaches is that of hedge accounting; FAS 133 and IAS 39 allow hedge accounting but the JWG approach does not. Hedge accounting is where an organisation has procedures in place to recognise that a certain derivative transaction has been transacted to hedge a particular economic transaction or anticipated transaction. There are effectively two types of hedge: a fair-value hedge where the gain or loss is taken to the profit and loss account with the gain or loss on the hedged item, and a cash flow hedge where gains and losses are taken to 'other comprehensive income on the balance sheet' until the hedged item is recognised. There are a number of tests to determine whether a hedge is allowable or not, and one of these is the test of 'effectiveness' where, broadly, 80 to 120 per cent of any gain or loss on the asset or liability being hedged should be matched by an opposite and offsetting gain or loss on the hedge instrument. However, there are a number of different calculations for the effectiveness test, and companies have to decide before the outset which method they will use and, once chosen, this method is not allowed to change. The reported results can be dramatically different; under one method a hedge may be 'effective', whilst under another it may not be. However, Finnerty and Grant (2002) recommend that the calculations should include a moderately large amount of data, for at least a period of twelve months, and that, where applicable, the forward premium should be excluded.

Where effectiveness conditions are met, hedge accounting allows for the deferral of the derivative gains and losses to the period of the realisation of the gains and losses of the underlying asset or liability (Creed, 2001). The use of hedge accounting recognises the 'matching concept' and may be useful to treasurers to smooth their bottom line earnings. Mueller (2003) examined the use of hedge accounting by 140 European firms that reported under US GAAP and thus complied with FAS 133. He found very little evidence that firms were using hedge accounting, and that the practice appeared to be that the companies either: (i) stopped hedging completely; (ii) hedged but did not use hedge accounting; or (iii) used hedge accounting for their use of derivatives. Of those using hedge accounting there were large differences between countries, with 30 per cent of companies overall using hedge accounting, varying from over half in the Netherlands to just 16 per cent in the UK. Thus, the impact of IAS 39 in the UK may have enormous consequences for UK treasurers that adopt IRR management strategies.

For example, if a company with floating-rate debt swapped into fixed-rate debt using interest rate swaps, under IAS 39 the swaps would have to be revalued to market. Under IAS 39 the swaps will be a cash flow hedge as the swaps hedge exposure to variability in future cash flows that are linked to floating rates such as LIBOR. The swaps would have to be shown on the face of the balance sheet at fair value, requiring continual revaluations to fair values. However, the floating-rate debt would have only small fair-value movements as the debt would always be close to market value. Thus, under the effectiveness test, the swaps may not qualify for hedge accounting, resulting in all the fair-value adjustments going through the profit and loss account rather than through shareholder's equity. A further complication is the matter of taxation on these cash flows, but this complexity is beyond the scope of this research.

2.12 FRED 23 and FRED 30

In May 2002, the ASB introduced FRED 23 – Financial Instruments: Hedge Accounting – to become mandatory for companies in 2003. This was followed in June 2002 by FRED 30 – Financial Instruments: Disclosure and Presentation, Recognition and Measurement. The introduction of these proposals had not been popular as they were similar to IAS 32 and IAS 39, apart from the notion of 'recycling', and most companies would have needed to set up new information systems to comply with FRED 23 and then change them again to meet IAS 39 requirements. Arguably, preparers were unhappy about implementing a new standard for just one, or possibly two years. From a corporate governance standpoint, the profession needs to restore faith in the financial statements, and the constant changing of demands on management and the change to year-on-year comparisons are unlikely to achieve that objective (Raeburn and Boyle, 2002).

One reason why these new accounting standards are so important is that many UK-listed companies use derivative instruments, such as interest rate swaps, to manage their financial risks. However, the many arguments in the press and by commentators about the correct way to go forward in accounting for financial instruments may have a heavy influence on the management of IRR by UK treasurers. De Marzo and Duffie (1995) had some years earlier documented that an accounting policy on derivatives disclosure could influence corporate hedging decisions. Chacko, Tufano and Verter (2001) agreed, arguing that the accounting treatment of derivatives occasionally discouraged firms from engaging in risk management. Thus, the final research question in this study seeks to examine what effect, if any, these standards will have on corporate treasury departments, and thus seeks to inform future policy.

2.13 Summary

This chapter has raised a number of issues that are of interest to the examination of IRR within organisations. From this discussion, nine research questions have been raised that are addressed in the empirical chapters of this monograph. In particular, the monograph seeks to investigate whether IRR is: (i) important to all UK companies, irrespective of size; (ii) actively managed by UK companies with the establishment of a clear IRR policy; (iii) important to companies with different equity, funding and gearing structures; (iv) dependent upon the same factors in all firms; (v) managed differently depending upon forecasts of future interest rates, inflation rates, yield curve movements or a combination of factors; (vi) more important than FX rate risk; (vii) managed through the use of derivative products, especially using interest rate swaps; (viii) monitored at board level such that corporate governance is maintained with effective monitoring, reporting and control guidelines; and (ix) likely to change as the IAS's environment changes.

This Page is Intentionally Left Blank

3

Research Method

This Page is Intentionally Left Blank

3.1 Introduction

Many reasons have been advanced to explain why corporate treasurers use swaps and other derivative instruments. However, most of these studies are either normative in nature or adopt quantitative methods using large financial databases to test hypotheses. Consequently, the substantive literature in this area rarely adopts a more qualitative approach to examine the motives of participants directly. For example, Titman (2002) commented that:

> we would like to have more insights on what corporate treasurers and CFO's do and think about on a day-to-day basis.

This study, therefore, adopts a more qualitative approach and explores how important UK treasurers consider IRR to be for their companies and how they manage such risk on a daily basis. Thus, the research methods adopted in this monograph were interviews with treasurers and a questionnaire survey.

3.2 Interviews

The research approach adopted in this study involved visits to ten organisations in the UK where typically the treasurer was interviewed; details of the industries that these companies operated in are provided in Table 3.1. The companies in the sample were selected because they were located in different geographical areas, operated in a variety of industrial sectors and represented small,

Table 3.1: List of interviewees

Interviewee	*Location*	*Sector*
A	London and South East	Food
B	London and South East	Tobacco
C	London and South East	Drinks and leisure
D	Scotland	Utility
E	Scotland	Drinks and leisure
F	Scotland	Transport
G	London and South East	Engineering
H	Rest of England	Manufacturing
I	London and South East	Telecommunications
J	London and South East	Property

medium and large organisations. The sample, therefore, represents a broad range of organisations in the UK and the results obtained should not be specific to any one sub-group of companies.

Semi-structured questionnaires were used for these interviews, which lasted for approximately one hour. Each interview was conducted by two members of the research team and all were recorded; detailed notes were also taken. One member of the team attended all of the interviews to supply a common perspective on the interview responses and to facilitate a comparison of the responses to the common questions asked.

3.3 Questionnaires

Two questionnaires (A and B) were prepared and the sample companies were sent one or the other, at random. This was because a single questionnaire would have been too lengthy and might have negatively affected the response rate (Helliar *et al.*, 2002b; Burton, Helliar and Power, 2003). Both questionnaires contained a large and varied number of questions, although there were a number of questions common to both. Some of the questions were open-ended, while others required respondents to select an answer from a menu of available options. Most of the questions employed Likert scales. The questions included in the questionnaire were drawn from two main sources: (i) the existing literature on the subject; and (ii) the findings of the interviews with corporate treasurers.

Table 3.2 shows that a total of 564 questionnaires were posted in May 2003; 288 companies were posted questionnaire A and 276 companies were sent questionnaire B. The samples were selected randomly from a listing of the non-financial FTSE 350 firms, other listed companies and AIM. The total sample consisted of 136 of the FTSE 350 non-financial firms, 353 other listed companies and 75 AIM-listed companies. This selection of companies was used to obtain the views of a variety of companies of different sizes from a range of sectors. A second mailing was sent out a few weeks later to those who had not returned their questionnaires. This second mailing included another copy of the questionnaire and a letter to be completed by the respondents if they

Table 3.2: A Summary of the questionnaire responses

	FTSE 350	*Other*	*AIM*	*Total*
Number of questionnaires sent				
Questionnaire A	71	176	41	288
Questionnaire B	65	177	34	276
Total	136	353	75	564
Number of completed questionnaires received				
Questionnaire A	39 (55%)	42 (24%)	4 (10%)	85 (30%)
Questionnaire B	32 (49%)	44 (25%)	5 (15%)	81 (29%)
Total	71 (52%)	86 (24%)	9 (12%)	166 (29%)

did not intend to answer the questionnaire, outlining the reasons for their decision.

An analysis of Table 3.2 reveals that 166 usable questionnaires were returned; eighty-five replied to questionnaire A and eighty-one responded to questionnaire B. This set of returns gives a usable response rate of 29 per cent, which is a good response rate for questionnaires on this type of topic (Burton, Helliar and Power, 2003). The table shows that the response rate of over 50 per cent for the FTSE 350 was exceptional. The response rate of 24 per cent for the rest of the Official List (Other) was closer to other survey response rates, while the corresponding rate for the AIM-listed companies was less than 15 per cent. The FTSE 350 response rate may show that IRR is a topic that is of great importance to large companies, and they were, therefore, interested in replying to this survey. The responses from the smaller AIM-listed companies was very small with just nine replies in total from these companies, giving a response rate of 10 per cent for questionnaire A and 15 per cent for questionnaire B.

An analysis of the reasons for non-participation (Table 3.3) shows that even though only a small number of AIM companies completed the questionnaires, another 41 per cent responded with an explanation for their lack of participation. Half of these companies indicated that they did not have any IRR or did not actively manage this risk. This may in part be because smaller companies prioritise sorting out their basic business, strategy and operations before they worry about the niceties of financial risk management (Helliar *et al.*, 2002b). In contrast, close to 40 per cent of the FTSE

Table 3.3: Non-respondent data

Description	FTSE 350	Number Other	AIM
No significant IRR/do not actively manage IRR	4	28	15
Company policy not to participate	8	26	6
Too busy	2	6	4
Too small	0	0	3
Other reason	2	11	3
Total	16	71	31
Response rate (%)	12	20	41

350 and 'Other firms' who provided reasons for non-participation explained that it was company policy that had prevented them from answering the questionnaire.

Questionnaires A and B were fairly similar. Questionnaire A had six sections, over seven pages comprising: (i) background information; (ii) IRR policy; (iii) funding and forecasting; (iv) perceptions of IRR management; (v) IRR management and derivatives; and (vi) accounting standards. Questionnaire B also had six sections covering seven pages and comprised: (i) background information; (ii) treasury management; (iii) IRR policy; (iv) funding; (v) IRR exposure; and (vi) IRR management and derivatives. The sections on background information, IRR policy, IRR management and derivatives, and most of the funding/funding and forecasting sections were identical in both questionnaires. Thus, there were many questions common to both questionnaires, with two sections in each that were unique.

To ensure that the responses from these questionnaires were generalisable to other companies, it was important to ensure that there was no difference between the respondent companies and the non-respondent companies. Tests were, therefore, undertaken to consider the effect of non-response bias by comparing the first mailing results with those from the second mailing (Wallace and Mellor, 1988; Hussey and Hussey, 1997). All of the responses between the two mailings were compared using the Kruskal-Wallis one-way analysis of variance. In total, there was a difference between the first and the second mailing for only

9 of the 248 questions[6], giving a 3.6 per cent rate that could not be ruled out on the basis of chance alone. Thus, it was decided that there was no response bias between the respondents and the non-respondents.

3.4 Analysis of the questionnaire responses

Chapter 5 reports the empirical findings using mean scores and standard deviations that indicate the responses of UK treasurers to the questions in the survey. The responses to the questionnaires were also analysed in a number of ways using cross-tabulations of the data, regression analysis, principal components analysis, and t-tests as well as trying to disaggregate the data based on factors such as size and sector. These findings are also reported in Chapter 5.

3.5 Summary

This chapter has summarised the research method that has been adopted in this study. The next chapter reports the findings from the first stage of the research in which interviews were conducted with corporate treasurers.

[6]In questionnaire A the questions were related to: (i) the maximum amount fixed up to one year; (ii) the more floating-rate finance, the less interest that is ultimately paid; (iii) buying exchange-traded options; (iv) selling exchange-traded options; (v) buying floors; and (vi) not using options under IAS 39. In questionnaire B, the three items were: (i) the number of years worked in the organisation; (ii) managing interest rates for future acquisitions; and (iii) how companies educate their treasury staff. Full results are available from the authors on request.

This Page is Intentionally Left Blank

4

Interview Findings

This Page is Intentionally Left Blank

4.1 Introduction

Ten interviews were conducted with a range of companies listed on the London Stock Exchange and on AIM, as well as one unlisted company. The companies operated in a wide variety of business sectors including leisure, manufacturing, property, raw mater-ials and services. The organisations also varied dramatically in terms of size, with sales ranging from the thousands to the multi-billion. However, most of the companies were very large, with sales in the billions. The exception to this were companies H and J, which were much smaller than the other companies. Nevertheless, these findings should be relevant to a wide range of businesses.

4.2 The importance of interest rate risk

The interviewees were first asked how they defined IRR, and unsurprisingly they tended to couch their responses in terms of identifying exposures generally. Two interviewees focused specifically on deposits and borrowings, whilst three interviewees highlighted the effect of IRR on the profit and loss account and on interest costs. Interviewee F (transport company) identified two dimensions to IRR when he defined it as:

> Our exposure to the volatility of the impact on both our cash flows and banking covenants from changes in interest rates.

Interviewee G (engineering company) was also worried about loan covenants and stated:

> [a] change in interest rates which would jeopardise either our financial covenants and/or our credit rating [which means that] it's the interest coverage that we put a bit more concern into.

The importance of the impact of changes in interest rates on earnings and shareholders' returns was encapsulated by interviewee I (telecommunications company) who stated that: 'it's the volatility to your earnings in general as well as the cash flow'. Thus, whilst no strong differences in definition were apparent, there was a variety of perspectives on the impact that IRR had on the financial performance of a company.

4.3 Factors affecting interest rate risk

The interviewees were also asked about the extent to which IRR affected their company. In general, it appeared that the perceived impact of any interest rate changes on the company determined whether an IRR policy was in operation and the key components of those policies. These policies were, in turn, often influenced by external perceptions of the company. For example, interviewee A (food company) claimed that:

> [The] interest cost is a fundamental issue that analysts always look at . . . anything that affects earnings per share is always quite highly focused on internally.

This perception was reiterated by interviewee G (engineering company) who noted:

> You've got to get your strategy right. You've got to be seen handling it [interest rate risk] properly.

Consequently, the interest costs *per se* appeared to be less significant to the interviewees than the volatility of the reported earnings arising from interest rate changes. Interviewee E (drinks and leisure company) believed that fixed-rate debt was ultimately more expensive than variable rate borrowings but that it had less impact on the volatility of reported profits. Thus, his treasury's main aim in their IRR policy was 'trying to protect [against] volatility'. Interviewee F (transport company) argued that if a company could 'stay floating you will always over a long term pay lower interest rates . . . than if you're fixed'. However, although he agreed that borrowing using floating rates was cheaper, his company did not have a 100 per cent floating policy. He explained that, due to the sensitivity of interest rate changes on earnings in his company, the 'set policy is to be approximately 50 per cent fixed/floating' although the amount of fixed-rate debt was permitted to fluctuate between 40 and 60 per cent. Interviewee C (drinks and leisure company) also supported this view when he stated that 'fixing long-term interest rates is counterproductive' as, although it gave certainty to costs, this certainty was obtained at a price.

However, the external perceptions of lenders were more important for some of the other interviewees. Interviewee B (tobacco company) summed up this perception by saying:

> [The] credit rating is vital to the firm . . . a problem with your covenants [is] really bad news.

Interviewee G (engineering company) was in agreement when he noted:

> [Our company's] main exposure in terms of adverse interest rate movements would be on its interest coverage ratios and thus on its financial covenants and thus on its credit ratings.

However, IRR management did not feature as importantly as the economic business cycle. His company's business followed the economic cycle quite closely and he claimed that interest rate changes affected 'our business less [so] than the general level of economic performance'. He, therefore, focused his treasury department's efforts very closely on trying to narrow the credit spread offered by lenders, reviewing the underlying rate of interest and argued that 'both have the same effect on your interest charge'. Thus, he and his colleagues spent a lot of time talking to bondholders, banks, life insurance companies, pension funds and insurance companies in an attempt to try to improve their credit spread in the debt markets.

In contrast interviewee F, in the transport industry, had different concerns, and concentrated more on capping the interest that was charged by fixing rates. He noted that:

> [We are] more concerned with capping interest rate risk [as the effect] is purely on the financial structure of the business . . . it's not on the operations [as] our underlying business streams are not sensitive to the economic factors which impact on interest rates.

Interviewee A (food company) was in the relatively unusual position of having only recently been employed to set up a treasury department on the auditor's recommendation. This, coupled with a high profitability ratio and large positive cash flows, meant that the company did not 'know as yet how exposed [they] are' to IRR influences on their global operations and other commercial factors.

In sharp contrast to company A (food company), interviewee H (manufacturing company) was the financial director of a company that processed a raw material that was at the mercy of world commodity markets. Consequently IRR was of little importance as

'95 per cent of earnings volatility is due to commodity price volatility'. A recent change of parent company, plus poor profitability, meant that the company had recently been forced to accept an asset-based financing arrangement by head office against their wishes and the lack of an IRR policy was the least of their problems.

There were a variety of responses about whether companies had implemented an IRR policy and these strongly reflected the specific circumstances of each organisation. For example, the profitable, cash-rich situation of company A (food company) meant that its IRR policy amounted to an investment policy for excess cash flows. This stipulated that managed funds should be used instead of using the money markets. In contrast, interviewee B (tobacco company) explained that they had a broad policy of fixing, on average, between 25 per cent and 75 per cent of debt for the next three years but that no hedging[7] beyond five years was permitted. He said that in general 'we try to watch the balance sheet' and, as the consequences to the company of a rise in interest rates were perceived as much worse than the benefits of a fall, they had chosen to fix a large percentage of their debt.

Interviewee C (drinks and leisure company) stated that they also essentially worked on a five-year time frame, moving from fixed debt of 25 to 50 per cent in year one to 0 to 15 per cent fixed by year five even though the IRR policy permitted fixed debt within the range of 25 to 75 per cent. In company C (drinks and leisure company), overseas subsidiaries remitted any excess cash to the central treasury department, which was based in the UK strategic headquarters of the company, and this was pooled together to pay external debt-providers.

Most companies had fairly liberal IRR policies which were operationalised more narrowly by the treasury department. This was highlighted by interviewee E (drinks and leisure company) who said that his company fixed 'between 30 and 70 per cent by currency' and that although this was 'quite a wide policy,

[7]When interviewees referred to hedging they were essentially talking about fixing their interest rates using a variety of derivative products.

[in] internal workings [it was interpreted] more narrowly'. He claimed that:

> You can either protect your shareholders' funds or protect your gearing, but you can't do both. The more on the gearing scale you get, I think the more you need to look at these things [hedging IRR].

Consequently the company hedged 'to protect the volatility of the bottom line'. However, he explained that the economic cycle was probably more important as the company was in the unusual situation that 'in a low interest rate environment we'd probably do slightly less better'. Thus, he believed that when times were good and the economy was booming, his company's products would be overlooked in favour of more expensive products offered by competitors.

In contrast to these rather narrow bands, interviewee G (engineering company)'s IRR policy was flexible but 'not . . . risky'. He explained that the financial director and treasurer each carried a lot of weight with the Board of Directors and that, if either of them considered that a change in policy was necessary, they would usually be able to persuade the Board to let them implement the change. Thus, a professional relationship, characterised by full communication from the treasury and finance function, appeared to be in place rather than a documented IRR policy that targeted a fixed/floating rate split in financing.

Both interviewees I (telecommunications company) and J (property company) identified the need for policies that could reflect and respond to both changes in the organisation and to the wider environment. Interviewee I (telecommunications company) noted that his company used to have very little debt, and as a result their debt's credit rating used to be AAA. IRR was, therefore, not a major issue, so the policy was just to have 'not less than 80 per cent fixed'. However, changed circumstances now meant that the company's IRR policy had changed dramatically. He stated that IRR policy was now:

> a compromise of tactical and strategic objectives [and] we can quantify the impact [of interest rate changes] and say [what] the cost is . . . it's a major risk now.

Interviewee J (property company) repeated similar concerns when he said:

> Interest rate management is a dynamic thing [which] changes as your expectations of the level of your borrowing moves.

His company had been in the unusual situation as a property company, of having variable income but fixed-rate debt, resulting in a profits fall when interest rates fell in 1997. However, fixed-rate debt was still not unattractive for the company as he explained:

> In 2000 we . . . fix[ed] 100 per cent of our expected borrowings for three years and 50 per cent of our expected borrowings for the two years after that.

Most interviewees returned again to the fixed/floating rate debt ratio when asked about the objectives of the IRR policy. Interviewee I (telecommunications company) provided an interesting view in declaring that the fixed/floating idea was too simple. He claimed,

> Companies will look at the competitor base . . . to feel that they are . . . within range. A company's attitude to fixed/floating is often very simply in terms of the risk it's prepared to take on the EPS . . . more floating gives a lot of volatility . . . which the city doesn't like.

Inquiries about the frequency of the review of the IRR policy highlighted various practices. For example, interviewee F (transport company) noted that his treasury operational strategy was updated weekly, but that this was approved annually by the Board of Directors. Interviewee B (tobacco company) said that his treasury department sent 'an overall gloss' of a treasury report monthly to the Board, whilst other companies operated on a rolling basis, reviewing annually.

The factors that appeared to influence the IRR management policy of these companies were the sector that they were in, the financial viability of the organisation and how soon there was a need to raise large sums of money. However, not all companies appeared to be as proficient as some of the others in understanding their IRR or managing it effectively.

4.4 Forecasting and the use of specialists

In an attempt to understand how companies assessed their IRR exposure, interviewees were asked whether they attempted to forecast interest rates, or whether they used other information providers' forecasts. This line of questioning elicited a range of responses; while some organisations relied on the production of in-house forecasts, others found the variety of research reports available from external agencies more useful.

There were six employees in interviewee E's (drinks and leisure company) treasury team and he explained that 'we all get individual bits of research', and thus the team assessed their IRR exposure using 'a bit of a mixture of mechanical elements but also a judgement call as well'. This 'judgement call' explained the hedging strategy adopted at certain times, with the amount that was hedged, depending upon their view at the time. Interviewees in other companies highlighted their use of economic research reports but as interviewee A (food company) said 'economic reports are very useful [but are] never right'. Interviewee F (transport company) expanded on this theme when he highlighted that:

> Electronic research reports and staying close to the market is more than enough . . . historic information is useful. Forecasts and analysts' views and brokers' views are pretty poor.

Most treasurers appeared to believe that the yield curve was the best predictor of interest rates, and factored this into any modelling they undertook. For example, interviewee E (drinks and leisure company) stated that:

> We tend just to take the forward rates at the time [from the yield curve]. We don't try to make any anticipatory decisions.

whilst interviewee B (tobacco company) confirmed that the 'yield curve affects where we go with our policy'.

Interviewee H (manufacturing company), who was more affected by the vagaries of commodity prices, simply assumed that interest rates would stay the same and appeared to find little relevance in yield curves. However, interviewee C (drinks and leisure company), who used the yield curve to calculate forward and spot rates and likely swap spreads, described a more sophisticated approach. He maintained that the shape of the yield curve was not as important as unpicking and understanding the curve to inform future IRR policy.

Interviewee B (tobacco company) maintained this theme when he detailed the context within which the yield curve was important. He elaborated that, for him, the important factors in assessing IRR exposure were: (i) the absolute debt level; (ii) the rate at which debt came down; (iii) the yield curve shape; (iv) their own expectations of the yield curve; and (v) the company's gearing level. He explained further that he used the yield curve more for management than for forecasting purposes. This idea of ranking issues that were important to the policy decision was echoed by interviewee C (drinks and leisure company) who said that the first question he asked when assessing IRR exposure was 'Have we enough cover?.'

It seemed that projected interest rates, however sourced, were regularly used for sensitivity stress-testing certain items in one or more of the financial statements and that Reuters and Bloombergs were used extensively. Interviewee I (telecommunications company) said:

> We have forecasts going for all years and we put in futures and swaps rates as a basis for budgets because we don't think you can really beat the markets over the long term.

He described how these forecasts and stress-testing were used when he noted that:

> We quantify the impact of one standard deviation, [and] two standard deviations by quarter.

A similar scenario was described by interviewee F (transport company) when he explained that they used 'three year forecasts for budgeting purposes' into which they factored 'currency rates and interest rates' where a view was 'taken on the forward curves'. Similarly, interviewee G (engineering company) explained that:

> All of our businesses produce budget[ed] forecast data . . . which go a few years ahead . . . and you sensitise those . . . we build consistent models [and provide descriptive] guidelines on the underlying economic assumptions.

However a contrasting approach was provided by interviewee H (manufacturing company) who said:

> We [produce] profit and loss account forecasts really to keep the banks happy. Because of the volatility of [our] market our forecasts invariably tend to be completely wrong, so it's not something we like to do other than when the bank says 'we need a copy of your forecast'.

Interviewee H (manufacturing company) produced three forecasts on spreadsheets – one with the commodity price they predicted, one with a worst commodity price scenario and a final one with a best commodity price scenario. In all cases they assumed that interest rates would remain unchanged. Interviewee E (drinks and leisure company) said that he assessed:

> What the overall interest charge is relative to what our operating profits are going to be [and] we do stress testing.

The magnitude and direction of interest rate changes were relevant for interviewee F (transport company) when he explained that: 'We do sensitivity [analysis] but no true value-at-risk.'

In describing his debt profile, interviewee J (property company) claimed that he would always have a fixed element of debt, a risk-reward element and a variable element. He said 'we hedge our profit and loss account and cash flow' and he expressed the opinion that this was much more important than hedging the balance sheet. Interviewee G (engineering company) summed up his approach by clarifying that:

> [W]e have a base debt forecast. Given that, and our existing interest rate structures, taking into account swaps etc, you have a base interest rate forecast, and of that you know that a percentage is fixed . . . We're prepared to accept more IRR in the further periods partly because we have no real idea what debt levels are going to be.

Despite the variety of views expressed about making interest rate projections, few firms reported using sophisticated treasury packages in their risk management as the functionality offered by modern spreadsheets seemed to meet most needs. For example, interviewee B (tobacco company) said: 'You can show a range of scenarios very easily on a spreadsheet.' However interviewee C (drinks and leisure company) was alone in using both Excel spreadsheets and a treasury system and 'Monte Carlo as a package'. Interviewee E (drinks and leisure company) explained: '[S]ome of the banks have software which we can access . . . but it's not something I've used.'

Thus, the forecasting of future funding requirements, debt run-off schedules and the projection of interest rates, credit spreads and yield curves all played their part in the activities of the treasury departments visited.

The use of advisors such as auditors, banks and brokers in the risk management process was discussed in the interviews, and a variety of practices were uncovered between the interviewees. Interviewee B (tobacco company) explained that, as his company often acquired other companies, they often took the advice of the acquisition advisor at the time. He added that banks were 'never backward' about their products, and other interviewees echoed this sentiment. Three interviewees mentioned that banks often provided ideas, research and alternative perspectives on economic factors to help them decide about market direction and IRR policies. Interviewee I (telecommunications company) explained that his treasury team comprised a member of staff who was undertaking a PhD in Finance, and that the practice and policy within treasury was improved by his 'academic ideas'.

Interviewee E (drinks and leisure company) noted that 'We don't pay advisors as such' but confirmed that their auditors had helped them with the new derivatives accounting standards. Interviewee B (tobacco company) also explained that they had sought their auditors advice on accounting for derivatives, but that they never asked their auditors for their advice on strategic or operational matters. Only interviewee C (drinks and leisure company) confirmed a role for auditors, beyond giving accounting advice, when he explained that their auditor provided comfort to the Board of Directors that treasury practice was 'sensible'. Interviewee C's (drinks and leisure company) unique situation was further evidenced by his revelation that every three years a team of consultants was employed to review and critique their treasury policies and operations.

Overall, the forecasting of these treasury departments appeared to be rather erratic, with no clear policy on the best way to distil all the data in the markets or to estimate the likely economic scenarios to help plan future hedging activities better.

4.5 The use of derivatives for interest rate risk management

All of the ten interviewees were questioned about the IRR management practices of their companies. In this regard, one line of inquiry sought to elicit information about the synthetic, or derivative, products used for IRR management. Responses to this line of questioning revealed that, with the exception of one company, all of the firms interviewed made fairly extensive use of a wide range of derivative products. For example, interviewee B (tobacco company) indicated that they 'use interest rate swaps, FRAs, caps, swaptions [and] floors'. Similarly, interviewee F (transport company) commented that his company 'use straightforward fixed-floating, floating-fixed swaps, we use caps and collars, [and] we use options'.

However, responses from the interviewees suggested that there was a clear preference for interest rate swaps over other derivative instruments; all of the companies interviewed used swaps to manage their IRR, while other derivative products such as FRAs, caps and collars were used to a much lesser degree. This finding that swaps were the most important instrument for managing IRR is consistent with the results obtained from previous research (see for example Bodnar *et al.* 1995 and Helliar 2004). The 1995 Bodnar survey into the derivative usage of US non-financial firms found that swaps were the 'overwhelmingly popular choice' among companies seeking to minimise their IRR; 78 per cent of companies which used derivatives listed swaps as their first choice among interest rate derivative instruments, while 95 per cent ranked them as one of their top 3 choices (p. 116).[8] However, although swaps tended to be the

[8]See also Berkman *et al.* (1997b) who found that swaps were the most prevalent interest rate derivative used by firms in Australia and New Zealand. Similarly, Howton and Perfect (1998) report that over 90 per cent of their sample of 451 Fortune 500/S&P 500 firms and 461 randomly selected companies used interest rate swaps.

instrument of choice for managing IRR among the firms interviewed in this study, one interviewee did note that the hedging strategies of his company changed according to its view of the market. In particular, interviewee C (drinks and leisure company) remarked:

> We choose to do different hedge strategies – that is, do swaps one day and swaptions the next and a cap the third. It depends on our 'gut feeling' about where interest rates are now, what value we're getting and where we think we are going to go. Where we are absolutely certain that interest rates are going to go up, and we think fixing forward gives us the best value, we will use interest rate swaps to lock in the rate. Where we are not at all sure whether interest rates are going to go up or down, but think they'll move sharply in one direction or another, we'll possibly use an option of some description.

The interviewees were also asked about their use of exchange-traded derivatives such as futures and options. Again, the responses were very clear-cut and suggested that, among this sample of companies, the most commonly used instruments were bank-arranged products such as swaps and OTC options. These products had the characteristic of being more flexible than their market-traded counterparts, and it would appear that companies valued this flexibility and favoured these products over exchange-listed and more rigidly defined products. For example, interviewee D (utility company) commented that exchange-traded products such as futures were 'too small and rigid for the company'. However, other reasons were advanced to explain the lack of preference for exchange-traded derivatives. In particular, several respondents indicated that they were unfamiliar with their use. In this regard, interviewee F (transport company) commented that 'I guess the real reason is that we've no experience of them.' In a similar vein, interviewee D (utility company) noted that his company was 'not staffed up for non-OTC'.

That companies may refrain from using certain types of derivative product simply because of a lack of knowledge has been widely reported in the literature (Bodnar *et al.*, 1995, 1998). By contrast, interviewee E (drinks and leisure company) indicated that his company had not explored the possibilities for IRR management that were offered by exchange-traded derivatives because 'we tend to be able to get what we require from the bank market'. This preference among companies for the flexibility that is offered by OTC instruments has been documented in previous literature which has investigated the IRR management practices of companies in the UK, the US, Australia and New Zealand (Batten, Mellore and Wan, 1994; Bodnar *et al.*, 1995, 1998; Holmes and Watson, 1995; Phillips, 1995; Berkman *et al.*, 1997a,b).

During the course of the interviews, respondents were also asked about any shortcomings that they associated with the use of derivative products. Although most interviewees appeared satisfied with the instruments available, some did comment on the costs involved with their use. For example, interviewee C (drinks and leisure company) commented:

> Sometimes we use collars, but not very often – a collar is two options and the bank is charging you twice – it's presented by the banks as no cost but it isn't.

Interviewee C (drinks and leisure company) further added that:

> the more complicated an instrument is, the more expensive it is. You should be able to take a [bank] package apart and see what value you are getting.

Most of the treasuries visited in this study had packages that allowed them to value the instruments that they were using and compare them with the terms that banks were offering them, and sometimes they did buy bundled option packages when the terms were considered to be reasonable. Interviewee E (drinks and leisure company) also remarked on the cost of derivatives products, but in terms of the administrative time involved in executing a transaction:

> There's the administrative cost in doing it on the day . . . time-consuming . . . and you have the ongoing administration where you have to make separate payments under that swap as opposed to the underlying borrowing.

However, notwithstanding these shortcomings, most interviewees were happy with the derivative products currently on offer, and indicated that there were no new and better instruments that they would like to see in the future. Interviewee F (transport company) summed up the availability of products as 'I think whatever you want is out there.' This sentiment was echoed by interviewee E (drinks and leisure company) who noted that:

> We have collars, we have caps, we have floors and things. So we have quite a lot of flexibility. I don't think we need anything else.

Interviewee D (utility company) went further in his assessment of the situation by stating that there is 'almost too much choice'. However, interviewee G (engineering company) was less certain of the adequacy of the current derivative products that were available when he commented that:

> One might occasionally wish for longer-dated instruments . . . or more liquidity in instruments.

although, this statement was tempered by his remark that 'I don't feel there are gaps in the market'.

Given the evidence that the interviewees made wide use of derivative products to hedge their IRR, respondents were asked how the treasury staff were educated about the hedging instruments available. This question elicited a mix of responses; while some companies relied solely on banks to provide the necessary education on hedging instruments, other companies used a number of different sources to educate their staff. For example, interviewee E (drinks and leisure company) commented that 'because most products tend to be variations on a theme', banks can provide the necessary education on derivative products. The idea that banks were an adequate source of information and education on hedging instruments was also supported by interviewee B (tobacco company), who remarked that: 'Any new information that has become available will be revealed by banks.' Interviewee D (utility company) also agreed that banks were a good source of information on hedging instruments, providing education free of charge. However, he noted that his company was a target for banks marketing products and, as long as his company was buying what the banks were selling, the banks were 'extremely helpful'.

Interviewee A (food company) sounded a note of caution about banks as a source of education, information and advice, when she said that although 'I get stuff from banks, I think that they are very biased towards their products – what you need is independent advice.' This view was echoed by interviewee F (transport company) who responded that: 'The banks are never backward in coming forward on products.' As a result of this aggression, and partiality, on the part of banks marketing their products, interviewee F (transport company) indicated that his company relied on a number of different sources to educate staff. In particular, he replied that his company educated staff about hedging instruments 'through the banks and I guess the ACT, the Treasury magazine, things like that.' By contrast, the situation at company G (engineering company) was markedly different. In particular, interviewee G indicated that the principal effort of his company to educate staff was directed at 'recruit[ing] ACT qualified people for treasury . . . because there is an awful lot of communication between treasurers and banks and people in the field'. However, the interviewee did admit that this strategy resulted in 'knowledge ebb[ing] and flow[ing] according to the circumstances of the company'.

Overall, there appeared to be a ready acceptance to undertake interest rate swaps, but not to investigate other hedging alternatives including interest rate options. Training also seemed to be random, with emphasis placed on the professional body of the ACT for guidance on key issues.

4.6 Corporate governance: Monitoring, reporting and control

One consequence of the large corporate derivative losses that have occurred in recent years is that significant attention has focused on the management oversight of derivatives activity (Dunne and Helliar, 2002).[9] Given this, interviewees were asked about the reporting and control procedures governing derivatives activity that were in place in their respective companies. Responses to this line of questioning revealed that the reporting and control of derivatives activity varied quite markedly from company to company. For example, while most of the sample companies had a documented policy regarding the use of derivative products, this

[9]For a summary of some of the scandals and insolvencies due to losses that have resulted because of derivatives usage, see Helliar and Dunne (2004) and Dunne and Helliar (2002).

policy was not always approved by the Board of Directors. In company F (transport company), the policy on derivatives usage was set out in a treasury manual, but it was more a 'code of best practice' and was not approved by the Board, as the treasurer noted:

> [We have] a treasury policies and procedures manual . . . It's updated annually. It's not really approved by the Board.

This situation differed quite markedly from company E (drinks and leisure company), where controls were widely used on the amount of derivatives transactions and the type of instrument permitted. Interviewee E (drinks and leisure company) explained that:

> We have, as part of the internal policy . . . what could be called an acceptable products list that are things that we can trade – defined types of instrument and defined maturities. So if we want to go out with that, then we have to go back and get further approval to actually do that.

In addition, internal controls were imposed on the nature of the counterparty to derivative transactions, as interviewee E (drinks and leisure company) explained:

> Our internal policy is single A or better . . . we tend to be in the double A's I think, but the official policy is single A or better – so some of the Japanese institutions we couldn't use.

This strict control of derivatives usage was also in evidence in company G (engineering company). In this company, treasury staff had some latitude in their use of certain derivative products, but the use of other instruments required the approval of the Finance Director or the Board as Treasurer G (engineering company) noted:

> We have freedom to use IR swaps and their equivalent . . . maturities up to 5 years and we will get the approval of the finance director before we buy an instrument . . . such as an option and we will not sell an option either unless it is equal and opposite of an existing transaction . . . or you've got a perfect hedge in another way. Anything else you have to go to the Board for.

Despite the varying controls on derivatives activity in the companies interviewed in this study, the pattern of reporting derivatives usage to the Board of Directors was similar. In particular, most of the ten companies interviewed indicated that derivatives activity was reported to the Board on a monthly basis. Interviewee D (utility company) explained that every month, as part of the management accounts, a range of reports were produced for the Board which covered the split between floating-rate and fixed-rate debt, the use of derivatives products, and also whether any deviations from the IRR management plan had occurred. This reporting process was similar to that of company G (engineering company), where he produced:

> A financing update monthly for the board . . . actually 10 times a year . . . anything from half a page to ten pages depending on what we're doing.

The situation in company F (transport company) was slightly different where, although the treasury department reported derivatives positions to the Board on a monthly basis, derivatives executions and trades were reported only semi-annually:

> We report to the Board monthly on derivative positions and semi-annually on derivative executions and trades.

The frequency of the reporting of derivatives activity to the Board of Directors amongst this sample of companies compares favourably to that documented for other companies in previous studies. For example, Bodnar *et al.* (1998) found that 50 per cent of the 399 US non-financial firms that they examined had no pre-set schedule for reporting derivatives activity, while another 17 per cent of companies reported this activity only annually. Only 27 per cent of the companies that they investigated reported to the Board either monthly or quarterly. Similarly, in a study of New Zealand firms, Berkman *et al.* (1997a) documented that a 'large' percentage of firms had no set schedule for the reporting of derivatives activity, although 61 per cent of the companies that they examined reported to the Board on a monthly basis (p. 72).

To further evaluate the degree of reporting and control that was exercised over the IRR management function, respondents were also asked whether their activities in this regard were monitored and evaluated. A review of the interview responses revealed that, in most of the sample companies, there was no monitoring mechanisms in place. Companies D (utility company) and E (drinks and leisure company) proved to be the exceptions. For example, interviewee D (utility company) explained that there were two main processes by which the hedging of IRR was monitored. First, there was a thorough annual review of treasury that was undertaken by the Board of Directors, and second, reports on IRR management activities were produced for the Board on a monthly basis. Interviewee E (drinks and leisure company) indicated that his company operated in a similar way when he described the monitoring and evaluation of the IRR management function as:

> What we do, on a monthly basis, is we present a mark to market to the treasury committee which goes to the management board and the main board as well. So, in effect, you can almost see the financial consequences of decision-making in the past.

However, a somewhat different situation existed in company G (engineering company). Interviewee G acknowledged that, in effect, IRR management activities were monitored, but he queried the value of this function:

> We test ourselves on these things . . . we produce regular reports . . . whether anyone reads them or not I don't know. I certainly don't think the audit committee does.

Of those companies where there was some procedure for monitoring and evaluating IRR management activities, the interviewees were asked further about whether the results from this process were used as feedback. In this sense, all the interviewees were in agreement that this tended not to happen and pointed to the futility of such an exercise. For example, interviewee E (drinks and leisure company) explained that:

> There tends not to be a retrospective [view]. Why did you do that? Why did you not do that? . . . You can't undo the decision later on . . . I think people say what's done is done, it's not really relevant to what you're doing now.

Thus, reporting and control differed between the firms, but generally there was an accepted procedure in place at each company, and treasurers worked around these procedures. However, the monitoring, reporting and control appeared to need enhancing in a number of the companies, and the corporate governance aspects were rather superficial.

4.7 The impact of accounting standards on interest rate risk management

Each interviewee was asked whether the hedging practices of their companies had changed in any way since the issue of the US standard on derivatives usage FAS 133 or FRS 13 which governs the disclosure of derivative and other financial instruments in the UK. In addition, the interviewees were asked whether any changes to their company's hedging activities were planned as a result of the requirement that all EU-listed companies must comply with IAS 39 from 2005. Interviewee D (utility company), the treasurer of a company that reported under US GAAP, was positive about the impact of FAS 133 and did not feel that the hedging activities of his company had changed in any way since its issue:

> We haven't changed things because of FAS 133. I don't think there are any transactions that haven't been done because of FAS 133.

Interviewee F (transport company) was of a similar view and opined that although the provisions of FAS 133 were very prescriptive, the work that was needed to comply with FAS 133 meant that the preparations required in order to comply with IAS 39 in 2005 were much less onerous:

> We comply with FAS 133 at the moment. And basically under FAS 133 we decided not to bother designating half our stuff as hedges because it was too prescriptive. And we are comfortable that the work we've done for FAS 133 to justify the commercial rationale for the hedges has put us in good stead for IAS 39 . . . . Our view is that the commercial rationale should drive it. But it's a very good check because if it doesn't meet the criteria then why did you do it as a hedge in the first place?

A contrasting opinion was offered by interviewee C (drinks and leisure company) who commented that much work needed to be done before they were in a position to comply with the provisions of IAS 39:

> Our documentation has got to be a lot better, as we will have to prove to the authorities that we are actually doing genuine hedges.

In addition, interviewee C (drinks and leisure company) commented that compliance with IAS 39 would affect their current hedging strategies because it would restrict the type of hedges that were permissible:

> We would like to do portfolio hedges . . . where we do not link a particular hedge to a particular asset (or liability), but this is in doubt now.

Interviewee E (drinks and leisure company) expressed a similar opinion when he commented that:

> There'll be 2 things. One is how to find the correct hedging mechanism to actually do it – and then where there are embedded derivatives – I think it'll be more difficult to justify them as a pure hedge.

However, interviewee E (drinks and leisure company) was more sanguine about the impact of IAS 39 on hedging activities. In particular, he thought that IAS 39 would 'affect the types of product that we use, rather than the overall strategy'. This view that IAS 39 would have a much greater impact on the hedging instruments used, rather than upon the actual hedging strategies implemented, was shared by some of the other interviewees. For example, interviewee B (tobacco company) assessed the impact of IAS 39 on the hedging products used by his company, explaining that:

> We sold some caps and some floors at about the same time and they both worked out really well, but we would no longer be able to get away with any form of hedge accounting for them, so we won't be using them again . . . even swaptions are probably a little bit in doubt because the mark to market is almost definitely going to be negative because of the optionality, so from day 1 you're getting a negative mark to market hit . . . a swaption wouldn't count as a hedge . . . you haven't got full control . . . so there'll be a little trouble because of that . . . we'll use mainly interest rate swaps in the future . . . you're really going to struggle to hedge account for anything else – apart from the purchase of caps.

One implication of the issue of FRS 13 is that companies are now in the position whereby they can obtain information on the hedging activities of their competitors; FRS 13 requires entities with publicly traded capital instruments, and all financial institutions other than insurance companies, to provide sufficient narrative and numerical disclosures regarding their use of derivatives and other financial instruments in their financial statements. Given this, each interviewee was asked whether they examined their competitors' disclosures on hedging activity, and whether this examination had, in any way, affected their own hedging practices. One general view to emerge from this line of questioning indicated that while the information was potentially valuable, it was far too complex to decipher. For example, interviewee B (tobacco company) claimed that 'it's the hardest note in the accounts to understand – definitely', before adding that:

> It makes me laugh actually – because you put all this information in, and if I struggle to work out what's happening somewhere else – ultimately, unless you get the detail, it's very difficult.

Some interviewees recognised the value of such information, but admitted that they tended not to look at the hedging disclosures of other companies because of a lack of competitors. This point was mentioned by interviewee E (drinks and leisure company):

> It's not something we do on an ongoing basis really. It's quite difficult to get true comparators.

Company D (utility company) was in a similar position and although this firm looked at the hedging of 'other companies, certainly', it did not look at companies in the same industry because it had no 'strict competitors'. Company F (transport company) was another company that did not focus on the disclosures of its competitors. However, interviewee F (transport company) advanced a slightly different reason for this, which effectively suggested that the disclosures made under FRS 13 were of limited value. In particular, he noted that:

> Typically, nobody [in our industry] really discloses what their band or policy is under FRS 13 . . . I think the range of disclosures under FRS 13 can be quite wide.

IAS 39 was still under review by the IASB, so until this was resolved, companies were working towards an acceptance of fair-value accounting and no portfolio hedging.

4.8 Summary

The findings from the interviews supported the previous literature outlined in Chapter 2. In general, companies believe in market imperfections and consider that it is in their interest to hedge against adverse movements in interest rates (Mian, 1996). These effects were seen to be relevant from a variety of different perspectives, including their impact on the companies' profit and loss accounts, balance sheets, credit ratings and in one case (the drinks and leisure company) the level of sales. In the case of the profit and loss account, specifically, companies were concerned with the effect of interest rate movements on overall interest charges, levels of, and volatility, in accounting profits and cash flows and/or interest coverage ratios. Balance sheet issues materialised in the form of implications for existing loan covenants and the disclosed earnings per share figures.

The treasurers interviewed believed that it was worth their while to manage their risk against unexpected movements in interest rates and were also willing to seek 'windows of opportunity' (Titman, 2002). In accordance with Ross (2002), the objectives of companies' treasury policies were defined in terms of acceptable gearing levels and fixed- to floating-rate ratios. Decisions on the proportion of fixed-rate debt were to some extent guided by the companies' forecasts of interest and inflation rates, the shape of the yield curve, any covenants that were in force and the length of periods for which companies intended to hedge.

Consistent with Bodnar, Hayt and Marston (1996) the interviews in this study revealed that most companies hedged their IRR with interest rate swaps, although sophisticated derivatives were also employed on occasion, in particular circumstances. Some interviewees were aware of the cost of these exotic derivatives and there was healthy scepticism concerning the propensity of banks to sell their own products.

In terms of the controlling and reporting practices for derivatives, most of the interview companies had procedures and policies in place to ensure stronger control over these instruments, but the extent and validity of these measures varied considerably amongst the firms. Some were sceptical as to their value, as there was often little feedback given to the treasurers. Consistent with the findings of Berkman *et al.* (1997b) and Bodnar *et al.* (1998) corporate governance aspects of treasuries could, in some cases, be improved. Finally, with reference to the implications of the new accounting standard IAS 39, respondent views were mixed. While one treasurer believed that the US standard FAS 133, that is similar to IAS 39, had not had a significant effect on their risk management approach, others viewed IAS 39 as curbing managerial choice in terms of the risk management strategy pursued as well as the risk management instruments used in the process.

Overall, the responses to the questions in the interviews gave an eclectic mix of opinions which made each organisation adopt a different view from other companies, depending upon their financial strength, their financial ratios, their areas of operation and their perceived future funding requirements. However the common theme to emerge from these interviews was that it appeared that funding requirements, as well as strategic and operational issues, seemed to affect the role, make-up and reporting obligations of the treasury department in each company.

This Page is Intentionally Left Blank

5

Questionnaire Survey

This Page is Intentionally Left Blank

5.1 Introduction

This chapter reports the findings of the questionnaire survey that was sent to UK Corporate Treasurers in May and June 2003. The findings of this questionnaire are possibly more generalisable to all companies than the findings of the visits to the ten different organisations discussed in the previous chapter, and may be helpful in summarising the perceptions of treasurers to IRR management.

5.2 Background information

In general, the respondents to the two questionnaire surveys covered a wide range of companies, in terms of size and industry, although the sample was skewed towards larger companies where 44 per cent had a turnover of over £1 billion and only 15 per cent had a turnover of less than £100 million. The industries represented by the respondent firms covered all sectors, including basic industries such as chemicals, construction and steel, consumer goods, industrials, information technology, retailers and the utilities. One-third of the respondents were in the cyclical services sector that covers the leisure industry, media and photography, retailers, support services and transport.

Over half of the respondents were treasurers and the rest were mainly financial directors or other accountants, where the usual length of service with their company was between one and five years. Most had a degree and a professional qualification. In terms of general financial risk management issues, 70 per cent of the sample had a treasury department that was normally staffed by between one and five people. In virtually all cases, IRR management was carried out centrally at head office by these dedicated treasury departments, and over three quarters of subsidiaries were required to borrow and organise their funding through head office.

In terms of the characteristics of the financing patterns of firms, only a third of the respondents had any credit-rated debt and, of these, over half had a BBB rating and just under a third had a single A; no respondents had an AAA rating. These ratings did not appear to have changed recently, but where there had been a change, it was generally downwards. Further, most firms had loan covenants placed upon them, often covering several different key ratios such as gearing and interest coverage.

5.3 Interest rate risk policy

About half of the respondents stated that they had a policy of setting ranges within which their fixed-rate debt had to be arranged. The longer the time horizon, the smaller percentage that had to be fixed. However, this did not change dramatically. For example, for one year out into the future, the minimum amount of debt that should be fixed was in the range 25 to 50 per cent, and the maximum was up to a 100 per cent. However for two or three years into the future, the minimum was still in the 25 to 50 per cent band, but the maximum became only 75 per cent. In just under 45 per cent of the respondent companies, these bands were set on a currency-by-currency basis regularly and in another 25 per cent such a system was used on an occasional basis. Thirty per cent set their target levels for their total borrowing without a breakdown by currency.

From these findings it appeared that companies could subject their risk management policy to a more independent review, perhaps by benchmarking against peers or hiring their accountants or treasury specialists to review their policies. Further, some companies could clearly enhance their polices by including currency factors and key ratios as well as the maturity and fixed/floating mix in the debt structure.

5.4 The debt and funding structure

There was a diverse range of respondent firms' gearing levels as measured by the debt to total net assets, varying from a level of less than 25 to over 100 per cent. Over half had gearing of less than 50 per cent, although 10 per cent of the firms had gearing levels of over 100 per cent. The proportion of debt that was fixed appeared to be in accordance with the policies that had been set, where most firms had the proportion of debt fixed in the 50 to 75 per cent bracket. From the interviews, it appeared that this current level of fixed-rate debt in firms' capital structures is higher than normal; firms have been taking advantage of the low interest rate environment that has characterised recent times, by borrowing at these historically low fixed rates rather than borrowing at floating rates that are likely to increase in the future. Often this proportion of borrowing at fixed rates had been set through the use of derivatives such as FRAs and interest rate swaps, as about three-quarters of companies used derivatives to change the fixed/floating profile of the groups' debt. This view was supported by the fact that these derivatives were often used to change the debt from a floating rate of interest to paying a fixed rate of interest, or to do both floating to fixed and fixed to floating at opportune moments.

Overall, these results suggest that firms are more likely to hedge in the immediate period, tapering down their required hedging levels the further into the future they look. Such practice possibly protects companies from large movements in interest rates in the immediate period and leaves some level of protection in the medium term, affording them the opportunity to benefit from favourable interest rate movements. These results are, in general, consistent with those that have been documented for FX risk management (Dhanani, 2003).

The financing strategies of the firms also varied in terms of bond funding and bank loans. For half the firms, less than 25 per cent of the total debt was through the issue of bonds, although some groups chose a strategy whereby nearly all of their borrowing was through the bond markets. The average term of the respondent firms' debt was medium term, in the four to seven year range although 10 per cent of companies had debt that matured in over ten years. However, derivatives were not used to change the term structure of debt. Thus, derivatives were used extensively to change the type of interest paid on debt, but not to alter other features of the borrowings. Debt was also only rarely raised using the method of securitising any income streams such as the rent on property leases.

Table 5.1 shows the profile of debt by currency that was used by respondent firms. Respondents were asked to rank the currency of their debt from the most widely used to the least used. These mean scores were the mean ranks on a score of 1 to 5, where respondents were able to reply to all five categories. Clearly, pound sterling was the most usual form of financing, closely followed by the US Dollar.

Table 5.1: Funding by currency

Currency	*No.*	*Mean*	*Standard deviation*
Pound sterling	150	1.793	1.089
US Dollar	115	1.930	1.167
Euro	110	2.464	1.627
Others	71	3.676	1.093
Yen	44	4.068	1.065

The Euro was also used widely, but other currencies, including the Japanese Yen were rarely used. Further, 68 per cent of companies indicated that sterling was their main or second most important funding currency, compared with 55 and 38 per cent for the US Dollar and Euro, respectively. By contrast, the Japanese Yen was not a funding currency at all for 74 per cent of respondent firms. The use of dollar and Euro financing perhaps reflects the level of international activity of the participating firms in the global markets, although it is surprising that the Euro did not take a more prominent role, possibly indicating that the US is still the main trading partner for UK companies. The Euro was used relatively little, and companies might change this as the UK progresses further its links to Continental Europe.

Respondents were asked about their use of derivative products to change the debt profile of their organisations. Currency swaps were used by about a quarter of respondents to change their debt profile by borrowing in one currency and swapping into another. However, the use of such a strategy was used less than the strategy of using interest rate swaps to change the fixed/floating interest rate profile of debt.

Companies, therefore, resorted to reviewing their fixed/floating mix rather than concentrating on the maturity profile or currency profile of their interest rate products.

5.5 Forecasting

Table 5.2 reports the responses to the importance of forecasts to IRR management. Responses were reported on a 5-point Likert scale with a 1 being very important, a 5 being unimportant and a

Table 5.2: Importance of forecasts

	No.	*Mean*	*Standard deviation*	*p-value*
The direction of interest rates	83	2.036	1.064	0.000
The magnitude of interest rate changes	83	2.193	1.064	0.000
Inflationary/deflationary trends	83	2.530	0.992	0.000
GDP trends	83	2.928	0.908	0.470
Industry trends and sectoral analysis	83	3.090	1.111	0.432

3 being neutral. Clearly, the direction of interest rates and the magnitude of interest rate changes were the most important. However, an analysis of the responses revealed that 81 per cent of companies viewed forecasts of the direction of interest rates as being important, with a mean response of 2.036, with forecasts of the magnitude of interest rates also being important with a mean of 2.193. Inflationary and deflationary trends were also important, but respondents were very neutral about GDP trends and industry trends, as reflected by the *p*-values that show these scores were not significantly different from the neutral score of 3. These forecast periods were usually estimated out to next year or two to five years in the future.

There appeared to be a reluctance of companies to look much further than two to three years ahead, and GDP and industrial trend data did not feature very often in the treasurers' data sifting. Companies could possibly focus on wider economic variables for a longer period of time in helping them determine their IRR management.

5.6 Factors affecting interest rate risk management

Table 5.3 reports the mean responses to respondents' views on their perceptions of IRR management. The mean scores reported are on a 5-point Likert scale where a 1 was strongly agree, a 5 was strongly disagree and a 3 was neutral. A visual inspection of the table shows that there were nine statements that respondents agreed with, which were significantly different from the neutral response of 3. These

Table 5.3: Factors affecting interest rate risk management

	No.	*Mean*	*Standard deviation*	*p-value*
Companies with overseas assets that are revenue generating will have debt in those currencies	79	2.215	0.779	0.000
The more floating-rate finance, the greater the volatility in the bottom line earnings figure	78	2.256	0.973	0.000
Highly geared companies, close to covenants limits, will have more fixed-rate finance	79	2.346	0.895	0.000
If the market predicts that rates will rise more than you think, any protection to hedge will be expensive	79	2.418	0.871	0.000
A company is more likely to manage its balance sheet if it is weak or it is approaching its banking covenants	78	2.449	1.002	0.000
If you think the yield curve under-prices interest rates, you are more likely to be fixed	78	2.474	0.864	0.000
The zero-coupon swap curve is useful	77	2.494	0.641	0.000
Analysts' forecasts of interest rates are poor	78	2.615	0.707	0.000
I am more likely to hedge if the yield curve is advantageous	78	2.709	0.963	0.000
If the yield curve is downward sloping, a firm is more likely to have a greater % of fixed-rate debt	79	2.861	0.971	0.206
The more floating-rate finance, the less interest that is ultimately paid	79	2.861	1.152	0.286
The Eurobond market is cheaper and easier to use than the US bond market	79	2.886	0.832	0.227
The recent credit crunch has resulted in companies using the bank credit market more than bonds	79	2.924	0.797	0.400
Yield curves are the best predictors of future interest rates	79	2.949	0.918	0.626
The bond market is cheaper to raise finance in and is longer term and less restrictive than banks	79	2.949	1.120	0.689
The yield curve helps to predict swap spreads	78	3.064	0.858	0.511

were that: (i) overseas assets are matched using the same currency debt; (ii) the more floating-rate finance, the more volatile the bottom-line earnings number; (iii) highly geared companies, close to covenant limits, will have more fixed-rate finance; (iv) hedging will be expensive if the market predicts higher rates than the company predicts; (v) companies close to banking covenants will manage their balance sheets; (vi) if the yield curve under-prices interest rates, more fixed-rate hedging will occur; (vii) the zero-coupon yield curve is useful; (viii) analysts forecasts are poor; and finally (ix) hedging will occur more if the yield curve is advantageous. There were seven statements to which the respondents were neutral, including the fact that: (i) with a negative yield curve a company is more likely to have fixed-rate debt; (ii) the more floating-rate finance, the less interest that is paid; (iii) the Eurobond market is cheaper than the US bond market; (iv) the recent credit crunch has turned companies to the bank market; (v) yield curves are the best predictors of interest rates; (vi) the bond market is cheaper than the bank market; and (vii) yield curves help to predict swap rates.

A principal components analysis was performed on all the statements included in Table 5.3 for all the companies, but the results did not provide any satisfactory explanations. However, when just the large companies were examined there were six dominant eigenvalues (with values over 1) as shown in Tables 5.4 and 5.5. From Table 5.5, the six factors appeared to be: PC1, using the yield curve to fix rates; PC2, closeness to covenants will result in balance sheet management and the use of the bond market; PC3, floating-rate finance is cheaper; PC4, analysts' forecasts are poor; the usefulness of the zero-coupon yield curve (PC5) and the use of the yield curves to predict rates (PC6).

Table 5.4: Eigenvalues of large companies

Component	*Eigenvalue*	*% of variance*	*Cumulative %*
1	2.672	16.7	16.7
2	2.131	13.3	30.0
3	1.881	11.8	41.8
4	1.486	9.3	51.1
5	1.266	7.9	59.0
6	1.094	6.8	65.8

Table 5.5: Principal components

	PC1	*PC2*	*PC3*	*PC4*	*PC5*	*PC6*
If the yield curve is downward sloping, a firm is more likely to have a greater % of fixed-rate debt	0.642	0.049	−0.241	−0.261	0.098	−0.218
Yield curves are the best predictors of future interest rates	0.073	−0.163	−0.524	0.371	0.408	0.116
The yield curve helps to predict swap spreads	0.227	0.489	−0.191	−0.262	−0.167	0.564
The zero-coupon swap curve is useful	−0.021	0.404	−0.385	−0.187	−0.628	−0.214
I am more likely to hedge if the yield curve is advantageous	0.723	−0.283	0.085	−0.096	−0.087	−0.013
Analysts' forecasts of interest rates are poor	0.011	0.443	0.154	0.537	0.009	−0.116
The more floating-rate finance, the less interest that is ultimately paid	0.108	−0.049	0.712	−0.317	0.213	0.417
The more floating-rate finance, the greater the volatility in the bottom-line earnings figure	0.495	−0.287	0.015	0.465	0.177	−0.137
If you think the yield curve under-prices interest rates, you are more likely to be fixed	0.778	−0.098	−0.056	0.016	−0.341	−0.078
If the market predicts that rates will rise more than you think, any protection to hedge will be expensive	0.531	−0.211	0.282	−0.324	0.099	−0.297
A company is more likely to manage its balance sheet if it is weak or it is approaching its banking covenants	0.113	0.622	0.330	0.295	−0.203	−0.056
Highly geared companies, close to covenants limits, will have more fixed-rate finance	0.238	0.474	0.530	0.027	0.118	−0.224
Companies with overseas assets that are revenue generating will have debt in those currencies	0.563	0.239	−0.218	0.440	−0.054	0.359
The bond market is cheaper to raise finance in and is longer term and less restrictive than banks	0.683	0.659	−0.021	−0.046	0.461	−0.211
The Eurobond market is cheaper and easier to use than the US bond market	0.380	0.147	−0.219	−0.194	0.266	0.302
The recent credit crunch has resulted in companies using the bank credit market more than bonds	0.036	−0.402	0.506	0.369	−0.338	0.227

Table 5.6 reports the mean scores to a number of different situations that might be important to companies in their IRR management programmes. Surprisingly, there were only three factors that

Table 5.6: Why companies manage interest rate risk

	No.	*Mean*	*Standard deviation*	*p-value*
To manage reported profits	73	2.343	0.885	0.000
It protects shareholder funds	72	2.512	1.048	0.000
The interest charge to EBIT/EBITDA is significant	73	2.644	1.06	0.005
The interest charge to EPS is significant	72	2.792	1.060	0.100
It has a high interest charge relative to operating profit	73	2.904	1.120	0.467
The balance sheet structure requires managing	73	2.930	0.900	0.512
It has a high absolute level of borrowing	72	2.944	1.197	0.695
To manage possible future acquisitions	72	2.958	0.971	0.717
It protects gearing	72	3.028	0.978	0.810
It is close to its banking covenants	73	3.041	1.047	0.738
Reported profits are sensitive to interest rate changes	72	3.042	1.054	0.738
The business is affected greatly by the economic cycle	73	3.096	1.056	0.440
Cash-flow streams are sensitive to interest rate changes	73	3.110	1.035	0.369
It reduces credit risk	73	3.151	0.953	0.181
To minimise tax payments	73	3.164	0.928	0.135
To implement an intensive capital spending programme	72	3.347	0.966	0.003
To maintain a high dividend payout ratio	71	3.409	0.888	0.000
Remitted profits are sensitive to interest rate changes	72	3.444	0.933	0.000
It has a slow rate of debt repayment	73	3.466	0.973	0.000
It has poor financial ratios	57	3.493	0.988	0.000
The business is likely to change fundamentally	73	3.521	0.974	0.000
Market value of assets is sensitive to interest rate changes	73	3.671	0.944	0.000
The chance of a credit downgrade is high	73	3.740	0.972	0.000
Book value of assets is sensitive to interest rate changes	73	3.753	0.847	0.000

appeared to be important to respondents: to manage reported profits; to protect shareholder funds; and where the interest charge to EBIT/EBITDA was significant. There were twelve factors where the respondents were neutral about whether the factor was important, including: a high absolute level of debt; high gearing; close to banking covenants; and to minimise tax payments. The neutrality of some of these findings is surprising, as it is normally expected that a company with high gearing or close to its covenants would adopt IRR management policies. There were nine factors that respondents did not think important at all including: the maintenance of a high dividend payout ratio; poor financial ratios; and a high chance of a credit downgrade.

These twenty-four factors were analysed using principal components analysis and Table 5.7 shows all those factors with an eigenvalue greater than 1. These six components explain nearly three-quarters of the variation in the data. Table 5.8 provides a summary of these factors. In particular, the table shows that the six factors are: (i) financial distress proxies (PC1); (ii) tax incentives (PC2); (iii) business strategy (PC3); (iv) managing the bottom line (PC4); (v) covenants (PC5); and (vi) future opportunities (PC6). Thus, these twenty-four factors can be distilled into six features that may explain respondents' views to IRR management. Obviously, companies in financial difficulties may wish to adopt a strategy to minimise any volatility to interest rate exposure. Similarly, the existence of loan covenants may also affect the risk management strategies adopted. Thus, there appear to be intuitively satisfactory explanations for these views.

Table 5.7: Eigenvalues

Component	*Eigenvalue*	*% of variance*	*Cumulative %*
1	9.178	38.2	38.2
2	2.769	11.6	49.8
3	1.656	6.9	56.7
4	1.519	6.3	63.0
5	1.193	5.0	68.0
6	1.108	4.6	72.6

Table 5.8: Principal components

	PC1	*PC2*	*PC3*	*PC4*	*PC5*	*PC6*
It is close to its banking covenants	0.638	−0.321	0.290	0.042	0.469	0.073
It has poor financial ratios	0.779	−0.248	0.281	−0.009	0.278	0.114
It has a high absolute level of borrowing	0.676	−0.432	0.016	−0.121	0.394	−0.035
It has a slow rate of debt repayment	0.696	−0.313	−0.017	−0.232	0.009	0.108
It has a high interest charge relative to operating profit	0.672	−0.544	−0.083	0.060	0.051	−0.051
The balance sheet structure requires managing	0.570	−0.104	0.166	0.200	−0.167	−0.455
The interest charge to EPS is significant	0.645	−0.359	0.203	0.185	−0.373	−0.166
The interest charge to EBIT/EBITDA is significant	0.739	−0.427	−0.123	0.093	−0.276	−0.040
The chance of a credit downgrade is high	0.597	−0.021	0.345	−0.210	−0.086	−0.195
The business is affected greatly by the economic cycle	0.573	0.019	0.193	0.202	−0.363	0.493
The business is likely to change fundamentally	0.461	0.074	0.554	0.154	−0.290	0.455
It protects shareholder funds	0.507	0.069	−0.378	0.432	−0.110	−0.224
It protects gearing	0.777	−0.014	−0.018	0.250	0.034	−0.119
It reduces credit risk	0.639	0.002	0.259	0.103	0.063	−0.142
To manage reported profits	0.382	0.365	−0.227	0.541	0.004	0.160
To manage possible future acquisitions	0.418	0.564	0.153	0.368	0.310	0.087
To minimise tax payments	0.314	0.766	0.228	0.095	0.119	−0.248
To implement an intensive capital spending programme	0.487	0.481	0.044	−0.254	−0.074	−0.098
To maintain a high dividend payout ratio	0.630	0.363	−0.040	0.015	0.094	−0.159
Book value of assets is sensitive to interest rate changes	0.704	0.248	0.013	−0.379	−0.230	−0.092
Market value of assets is sensitive to interest rate changes	0.742	0.279	−0.010	−0.450	−0.154	−0.035
Cash-flow streams are sensitive to interest rate changes	0.654	0.244	−0.459	−0.143	0.080	0.243
Remitted profits are sensitive to interest rate changes	0.667	0.301	−0.242	−0.355	0.005	0.152
Reported profits are sensitive to interest rate changes	0.587	0.003	−0.574	−0.007	0.214	0.211

5.7 The importance of interest rate risk versus exchange rate risk

A key question addressed by this study is the importance of IRR management in UK firms. The survey, therefore, asked respondents how important certain economic factors were for their firms. Table 5.9 shows that 21 of the 26 items were important to the surveyed companies, with means below 3 on a 5-point Likert scale, where a 1 was important and a 5 unimportant. The most important factors were UK base-rate changes and the exchange rate for pound sterling, all with means below 2. This finding demonstrates that, despite the globalisation of world

Table 5.9: The importance of various economic variables

Risk	*No.*	*Mean*	*Standard deviation*	*p-value*
UK base-rate rises	79	1.823	0.781	0.000
UK base-rate falls	78	1.846	0.701	0.000
UK£ exchange rate strengthening	79	1.962	0.940	0.000
UK£ exchange rate weakening	79	1.962	0.884	0.000
US$ exchange rate weakening	77	2.169	1.056	0.000
US$ exchange rate strengthening	77	2.182	1.035	0.000
Euro exchange rate strengthening	78	2.218	0.989	0.000
Inflation rates rising	78	2.256	0.763	0.000
Deflation	78	2.256	0.829	0.000
Euro exchange rate weakening	77	2.270	0.976	0.000
Inflation rates falling	78	2.372	0.824	0.000
US$ interest rate rises	79	2.494	1.218	0.000
Positive yield curve steepening	75	2.507	0.844	0.000
US$ interest rate falls	78	2.525	1.214	0.001
Euro currency interest rate rises	78	2.526	1.113	0.000
Euro currency interest rate falls	79	2.531	1.119	0.000
Negative yield curve steepening	75	2.533	0.811	0.000
Yield curve flattening	75	2.547	0.826	0.000
Other raw material price increases	77	2.623	1.077	0.003
Credit spreads widening	75	2.627	0.969	0.001
Credit spreads narrowing	76	2.697	0.952	0.007
Oil price increases	77	2.766	1.297	0.118
Other exchange rates strengthening	78	2.920	1.067	0.521
Other exchange rates weakening	76	2.948	1.087	0.676
Other currency interest rate rises	75	3.240	1.172	0.080
Other currency interest rate falls	75	3.253	1.626	0.063

trade, UK economic features are the most important economic indicators for UK companies. The next most important factor was the US rate of exchange, perhaps as a result of the US representing an important trading partner to the UK and/or a large proportion of commodities being priced in US Dollar terms. This situation may change if the UK joins the Euro. Following on from the significance of the US rate of exchange, companies were also more concerned with changes to interest rates in the US; changes to the Euro interest rates followed. There were three factors that respondents were neutral about: other exchange rates either strengthening or weakening and oil price increases. Increases and decreases in the interest rate[10] of other currencies were not considered important; over a third of the respondents claimed that such movements were not important at all.

A principal components analysis was also conducted on the twenty-six factors in Table 5.9. Table 5.10 shows that there were seven factors with eigenvalues above 1 that explain just over 85 per cent of the data. Table 5.11 describes these seven factors in detail. In particular, the important factors were identified as: US Dollar and other currency interest rate changes; inflation and deflation; the Euro currency interest rate and exchange rate; the UK base rate; the Euro and other currency interest rates; inflation and oil price decreases. The overall conclusion from these factors

Table 5.10: Eigenvalues

Component	*Eigenvalue*	*% of variance*	*Cumulative %*
1	1.955	30.6	30.6
2	4.896	18.8	49.4
3	2.993	11.5	60.9
4	2.214	8.5	69.4
5	1.769	6.8	76.2
6	1.214	4.7	80.9
7	1.171	4.5	85.4

[10]At the 10 per cent level.

Table 5.11: Principal components

Risk	*PC1*	*PC2*	*PC3*	*PC4*	*PC5*	*PC6*	*PC7*
UK base-rate rises	0.296	0.383	−0.105	0.618	0.345	−0.177	0.292
UK base-rate falls	0.308	0.405	−0.110	0.570	0.256	−0.233	0.422
US$ interest rate rises	0.705	−0.241	−0.465	−0.100	0.177	−0.153	−0.209
US$ interest rate falls	0.721	−0.233	−0.442	−0.068	0.174	−0.168	−0.197
Euro currency interest rate falls	0.323	0.115	0.772	−0.133	0.395	−0.101	−0.134
Euro currency interest rate rises	0.340	0.111	0.746	−0.139	0.417	−0.118	−0.076
Other currency interest rate rises	0.743	−0.240	−0.059	−0.296	0.424	0.009	0.202
Other currency interest rate falls	0.753	−0.240	−0.048	−0.293	0.410	0.014	0.190
Credit spreads widening	0.517	0.516	−0.002	−0.456	−0.174	0.066	−0.131
Credit spreads narrowing	0.551	0.528	0.000	−0.404	−0.178	0.051	−0.034
Yield curve flattening	0.673	0.528	0.009	−0.081	−0.198	−0.241	−0.076
Positive yield curve steepening	0.618	0.587	0.045	−0.109	−0.237	−0.310	0.029
Negative yield curve steepening	0.678	0.573	0.051	−0.101	−0.151	−0.271	−0.105
Inflation rates rising	0.232	0.738	−0.111	0.097	−0.024	0.490	−0.047
Inflation rates falling	0.301	0.719	−0.063	0.183	−0.006	0.447	0.070
Deflation	0.337	0.720	−0.066	0.208	−0.161	0.098	0.149
UK£ exchange rate strengthening	0.670	−0.331	0.271	0.362	−0.308	0.021	−0.179
UK£ exchange rate weakening	0.617	−0.327	0.306	0.330	−0.381	−0.020	−0.146
US$ exchange rate strengthening	0.621	−0.440	−0.461	0.228	−0.174	−0.084	−0.001
US$ exchange rate weakening	0.626	−0.460	−0.454	0.213	−0.159	−0.054	−0.043
Euro exchange rate strengthening	0.475	−0.385	0.610	0.213	−0.225	0.065	0.109
Euro exchange rate weakening	0.514	−0.374	0.627	0.245	−0.173	0.093	0.061
Other exchange rates strengthening	0.660	−0.404	−0.039	−0.297	−0.100	0.274	0.360
Other exchange rates weakening	0.667	−0.427	−0.046	−0.296	−0.088	0.298	0.314
Oil price increases	0.382	−0.008	−0.139	0.229	0.303	0.183	−0.540
Other raw material price increases	0.412	0.012	−0.036	0.344	0.389	0.384	−0.261

appears to be that interest rates are as influential to UK companies as exchange rates.

To examine the difference between the management of interest rates and exchange rates, treasurers were asked to indicate whether FX risk management was harder or easier than the management of IRR. In general, the respondents thought that both were equally difficult, although there was some indication that it was harder to monitor interest risk exposures than FX risk exposures, and to implement interest rate policy documentation and strategies. Overall, management of IRR in UK companies represented an important financial activity for two reasons: (i) the significance of movements in interest rates; and (ii) the technical difficulties associated with the management of these interest rate changes.

The companies were asked whether they used any methods to assess their interest rate exposure and the frequency with which they used them. Stress-testing was the most frequently used technique, used either on an 'often' basis or on a 'sometimes' basis (Table 5.12). The other techniques, with scores of close to or more than 4 were used only on rare occasions. These results are surprising as some of these methods, such as gap analysis and duration analysis, have been established for a long time and the value-at-risk model has had wide coverage. In the interviews, however, the treasurers indicated that they relied on their own spreadsheets and specialist packages for analysing their exposures, and some of these packages may have incorporated these techniques without necessarily mentioning them by name.

Table 5.12: Assessment of interest rate risk policy

	No.	*Mean*	*Standard deviation*
Stress-testing	66	3.667	1.363
Gap analysis	66	3.955	1.397
Duration analysis	65	3.955	1.419
Value-at-risk	63	4.191	1.242
Simulations (e.g. Monte Carlo)	65	4.508	0.886
Other (please state)	16	4.625	1.088

5.8 Interest rate risk management and the use of derivatives

Most of the respondents stated that they made no attempt to use internal strategies to help manage their IRR. These results are surprising as internal strategies are, by their very nature, cheaper to implement than external methods and the FX risk management literature covers a number of different internal hedging strategies including netting and matching (Dhanani, 2003). However, prior research into the management of FX risk also suggests that external strategies normally dominate (Davis *et al.*, 1991).

Table 5.13 reports the extent to which certain derivative instruments are used to hedge IRR. The question was framed as a 5-point Likert scale where a 1 was 'always' and a 5 was 'never'. Interest rate swaps were clearly the most often-used product, with a mean score of 2.506, demonstrating that most respondents often used this product. FRAs and caps were sometimes used, with mean a score of 3.497. All of the other products listed in the questionnaires, such as collars, floors, futures and options were either only rarely used or

Table 5.13: The derivative products used

	No.	*Mean*	*Standard deviation*
Interest rate swaps	158	2.506	1.276
Forward rate agreements	153	3.497	1.231
Buying caps	150	3.880	1.029
Buying collars	149	4.114	0.941
Buying interest rate options	149	4.275	0.958
Buying floors	144	4.347	0.895
Selling interest rate options	147	4.415	0.905
Buying structured derivatives	146	4.469	0.842
Buying swaptions	146	4.507	0.763
Selling floors	145	4.586	0.787
Selling caps	145	4.600	0.785
Selling collars	144	4.653	0.732
Buying interest rate futures	145	4.772	0.695
Selling interest rate futures	145	4.786	0.679
Selling exchange-traded options	144	4.847	0.492
Buying exchange-traded options	144	4.854	0.487

never used at all. This finding was particularly true for exchange-traded products. Interestingly, the standard deviations reduced as the means increased, showing that there was more general agreement about the non-use of exchange-traded futures and options than the frequent use of interest rate swaps. The interview findings also indicated the infrequent or non-use of exchange-traded products and a clear preference for interest rate swaps.

The use of swaps is unsurprising since swaps are one of the only medium- to long-term instruments available to hedge long-term maturity products such as bank loans and bonds, and this finding also supports other studies that show that interest rate swaps are widely used (Helliar, 1997). The use of FRAs is similar to that of the management of FX rate risk where forward contracts take precedence. The dislike of exchange-traded products also confirms prior studies (Bodnar *et al.*, 1995; Helliar, 1997), and reflects the fact that most companies like the flexibility of tailor-made products to suit their particular circumstances.

From the questionnaire responses, it was also apparent that the treasurers took apart the derivative packages offered by banks to analyse their value. Treasurers, it appears, are becoming as experienced as bankers in being able to pull apart and put together packages that are of use to companies in hedging their risk. The treasury staff also appear to use a wide range of sources to educate themselves about these products; including using the bankers themselves, professional magazines and professional bodies. Seventy-five per cent of the companies were also concerned with the credit ratings of banks, choosing not to deal with those with a rating of less than a single A. Surprisingly, however, a quarter of companies did not have any policy at all about the banks with which they could deal; these companies may wish to review their current policies.

A principal components analysis was conducted on the responses to the different instruments in Table 5.13 to see whether there were any reductions that could be made in the data to distil these different products. Tables 5.14 and 5.15 show the eigenvalues of the five factors that explain most of the variation in the data. Table 5.14 shows that these five factors explain nearly 80 per cent

Table 5.14: Eigenvalues

Component	*Eigenvalue*	*% of variance*	*Cumulative %*
PC1	6.332	39.6	39.6
PC2	2.396	15.0	54.6
PC3	1.517	9.5	64.1
PC4	1.203	7.5	71.6
PC5	1.131	7.1	78.7

Table 5.15: Principal components

	PC1	*PC2*	*PC3*	*PC4*	*PC5*
Interest rate swaps	0.372	−0.120	0.574	0.185	0.354
Forward rate agreements	0.386	−0.020	0.524	0.363	0.111
Buying interest rate options	0.807	0.052	0.076	0.236	−0.093
Selling interest rate options	0.798	0.067	−0.125	0.317	−0.021
Buying exchange-traded options	0.365	0.635	0.045	0.242	−0.434
Selling exchange-traded options	0.351	0.665	0.093	0.275	−0.392
Buying caps	0.619	−0.294	0.430	−0.254	−0.250
Buying collars	0.655	−0.384	0.374	−0.348	−0.211
Buying floors	0.713	−0.304	0.146	−0.313	−0.232
Selling caps	0.830	−0.156	−0.378	−0.074	−0.076
Selling collars	0.824	−0.115	−0.440	−0.062	−0.015
Selling floors	0.822	−0.113	−0.407	−0.077	0.026
Buying swaptions	0.695	−0.043	−0.109	0.236	0.376
Buying structured derivatives	0.615	−0.113	−0.039	0.161	0.425
Buying interest rate futures	0.369	0.746	0.113	−0.440	0.266
Selling interest rate futures	0.371	0.762	0.076	−0.414	0.285

of the results. An analysis of Table 5.15 shows that these five factors are: OTC options (PC1); exchange-traded derivatives (PC2); interest rate swaps and FRAs (PC3); the dislike of using interest-rate futures (PC4); and the preference for exotic option derivatives to exchange-traded options (PC5). The latter components tend to suggest that even exotic OTC options are preferred to standard exchange-traded products.

Questionnaire respondents were asked to write any comments that were applicable to IRR management. These comments revealed that most of the respondents were keen to use swaps in their treasury armour because they were simple and easy to use and understood by top management, confirming the attraction of the interest rate swaps market. Further, the comments made by the treasurers indicated that they were loath to use options, stating that they were too expensive, and did not like the upfront nature of the cost. The respondents also wrote comments that exchange-traded products were not utilised because of the daily cash calls and the inflexibility of the products.

5.9 Corporate governance: Monitoring, reporting and control

In terms of reporting derivative activity, a large proportion of firms reported to the treasury committee on a quarterly or monthly basis, but more worryingly, a third reported that they did not have a treasury committee.[11] A similar pattern was also found for the reporting of derivatives activity to the Board of Directors with a quarter of respondents reporting only yearly, or never, to the Board.

The majority of the respondents had a formal risk management policy which was reviewed either annually or on an *ad hoc* basis. This policy was generally reviewed either by the Board of Directors or the treasury or finance committee. Surprisingly, the Finance Director alone reviewed this policy in nearly a fifth of all companies. From a corporate governance perspective, about half of the companies involved non-executive directors in treasury policy, and about a quarter involved them sometimes, but a quarter never involved their non-executive directors in treasury policy. The audit committee was involved far less than the non-executive directors, with less than a third being involved on a regular basis.

In recent years, following the large derivative-based losses that have hit the headlines (Dunne and Helliar, 2004), the monitoring and control of derivatives usage has become an important part of treasury

[11] Possibly this was subsumed within a finance committee.

management. The responses to the questionnaires revealed that often the treasurer, but more commonly the Finance Director, had the primary authority for the use of derivatives within the policy framework; in over half the cases, the Finance Director bore the responsibility, thus hopefully strengthening the corporate governance processes within these organisations. However, control and reporting practices were probably the weakest area found in this research.

5.10 Accounting standards

The imminent implementation of International Accounting Standards, including IAS 39 in the UK, may have an important influence on the future of IRR management in UK companies, and thus respondents were asked about their practices in the light of current developments. Of those that answered this question, approximately 60 per cent of them stated that IAS 39 would affect their IRR management practices, and another 30 per cent stated that both IAS 39 and FAS 133 had affected treasury practice. An analysis of the instruments that may be used less in the future is shown in Table 5.16. This table demonstrates that there will probably be slightly less use of interest rate swaps and FRAs but that options and swaptions will definitely be used less. The use of futures will also decline, compounding their current unpopularity.

The attitudes to hedge accounting by respondents are highlighted in Table 5.17. This shows that two of the concerns about accounting standards will change risk management practices: if

Table 5.16: IAS 39 and its effect on the use of derivatives

	No.	*Mean*	*Standard deviation*	*p-value*
Forward rate agreements	57	3.158	0.527	0.000
Interest rate swaps	61	3.172	0.641	0.000
Interest rate futures	51	3.294	0.642	0.000
Options	61	3.541	0.787	0.000
Swaptions	57	3.632	0.723	0.000

Table 5.17: Hedge accounting

	No.	Mean	Standard deviation	p-value
'Hedge accounting' is disallowed	73	2.682	1.141	0.021
Gains/losses have to be 'recycled' through earnings	74	2.743	1.073	0.043
All items, including derivatives, are shown on the balance sheet at their fair values	74	2.811	1.081	0.137
Hedging on a portfolio basis is disallowed	73	2.863	1.058	0.272
Hedge accounting effectiveness is between 80 and 120% of the hedged item	73	2.904	1.056	0.440

hedge accounting is disallowed (as recommended by the Joint Working Group) and the requirement that gains and losses be recycled through earnings. These responses showed that treasurers were likely to change current practice, with means of 2.682 and 2.743 on a 5-point Likert scale. In addition, the *p*-value shows that these are significantly different from the neutral response of 3. For the other three situations cited, treasurers were more neutral: derivatives are shown on the balance sheet at fair value; hedging on a portfolio basis is disallowed; and the requirement that hedge effectiveness is between 80 and 120 per cent of the hedged item. This finding is slightly different from that obtained from the interviews which indicated that hedging on a portfolio basis was important to those interviewed.

Some respondents inserted written comments on the questionnaire before returning it. One comment noted by a respondent stated:

> I am fundamentally opposed to IAS 39. It is absurd that portfolio hedging is not permitted and absurd that derivatives are marked to market whilst the underlying debt isn't. Disclosure of market values under FRS 13 was perfectly adequate.

5.11 Regression analysis

A number of linear regressions[12] were performed on the data to examine in more detail the relationships between all the data that had been collected. These data was reduced using best-subsets to distil from the information any interesting features.

With regard to the use of derivative instruments, the regressions showed that the use of caps, collars and floors was related to whether there was an interest risk policy in place. Those with a policy to use such instruments were more likely to use them and it may be that a desire to use them precedes the policy. The use of swaptions was related to whether the company had any credit-rated debt, and the use of futures was dependent upon the sector and the focus of loan covenants.

The regression of the questions asking why companies managed IRR also revealed some interesting features. For example, companies with a high interest charge relative to profits normally assumed responsibility for risk management at head office. Those companies that managed their balance sheet structure tended to have more US Dollar and Euro financing, rather than just pounds sterling, reflecting the more diverse nature of their operations. The concentration on Euro financing, plus the size of companies, was also related to the possibility of future acquisitions, perhaps suggesting that companies are more likely to expand into Europe rather than the US, as has normally been the practice. Implementing an intensive capital investment programme was also related to financing in the Euro and other currencies, suggesting a move into Europe and other overseas destinations such as call centres in India or manufacturing plants in South East Asia, respectively.

Companies that had cash flow streams that were sensitive to interest rate changes appeared to have loan covenants in place and fixed-rate debt and those with reported profits that were sensitive to interest rate changes also had a high proportion of fixed-rate debt. These findings confirm the classic assumptions that imply that companies try to fix their debt levels when there is a chance of financial distress.

---

[12]These regressions are available from the authors on request.

On regressing the events that were important to companies, the amount of fixed-rate debt appeared to be important for those companies that were sensitive to UK base-rate changes, but the existence of covenants and the sector was more important to companies that were sensitive to US interest rate changes. The companies that were concerned about credit spreads changing had more credit-rated debt. The gearing of the companies seemed to be more related to exchange rate movements than interest rate movements with both pound and Euro exchange rates being sensitive to the gearing.

Finally with reference to the IAS 39, the analysis indicated that this standard will have the greatest impact on the use of interest rate options; 80 per cent of respondents who stated that IAS 39 would change their IRR management practice were currently using options, whereas the 20 per cent who indicated that their risk management practice would not change were much less likely to use options.

5.12 Cluster analysis and size

Some preliminary cluster analysis[13] was also performed on the data to establish any further relationships in the data. Unsurprisingly, the analysis showed that larger companies had larger treasury departments, but that mid-sized companies were less likely to have an audit committee involved in their activities. Larger companies appeared to be funded more by debt and thus had higher gearing, especially those in the £0.5 to £1 billion turnover category. These firms, in turn, also had more fixed-rate debt in their financing structure.

Company size also influenced managements' approach to the management of IRR. This finding confirms the results from other UK surveys that have also documented the importance of firm size (Burton, Helliar and Power, 2003). To examine in greater detail the impact that size had on the findings noted above, t-tests were performed on the data. Table 5.18 shows the difference for questions that were repeated in both questionnaires where there was a significant difference between the two size categories,

[13]These analyses are available from the authors on request.

Table 5.18: Differences between small and large companies: Questionnaires A and B

	Small		Large		*p-value*
Description	*No.*	*Mean*	*No.*	*Mean*	*Significance*
Years worked for the organisation	92	2.64	73	3.00	0.032
Position in the organisation	92	2.21	73	1.65	0.004
Is there a treasury department?	91	1.48	73	1.05	0.000
How many staff work in treasury	52	2.28	72	3.45	0.000
Is there any credit-rated debt?	88	1.85	72	1.33	0.000
Do subsidiaries borrow from the parent?	87	1.27	73	1.13	0.029
Is there an IRR policy?	90	1.20	73	1.01	0.000
Are derivatives used to change the debt profile?	89	1.40	73	1.12	0.000
Does the company pay fixed or floating or both?	56	1.82	65	2.38	0.001
What per cent of bond financing is used?	83	1.47	70	2.81	0.000
Is borrowing mainly in pounds?	80	1.55	69	2.08	0.003
Are borrowings swapped?	86	1.92	69	1.53	0.000
Are internal hedging techniques used?	86	2.52	70	2.24	0.018
Are bank packages taken apart?	86	1.55	67	1.28	0.001
What the lowest rated bank dealt with?	86	3.50	69	3.01	0.006
How are staff educated?	79	5.90	68	6.66	0.002
Are interest rate swaps used?	86	2.86	72	2.08	0.000
Are swaptions used?	81	4.67	65	4.31	0.006
Are structured derivatives used?	80	4.65	65	1.24	0.005
Who authorises the use of derivatives?	43	2.45	73	1.85	0.010
How often are derivatives reported to committees?	44	5.94	72	4.40	0.000

where large included those companies with a turnover of over £1 billion and small included those with a turnover of less than £1 billion.

An analysis of Table 5.19 shows that treasurers were more likely to have answered in the large companies, but financial directors were more likely to have responded to the questionnaire in smaller companies. This finding is confirmed by the size of treasury departments where smaller companies have just one person but larger companies employ between three and ten members of staff in treasury. Thus, in smaller companies the one person engaged in treasury activities was often the Finance Director that answered the survey. Larger companies were also more likely to have formalised treasury policies which were more frequently reviewed.

Smaller companies were less likely to have any credit-rated debt, possibly because smaller firms do not have the resources to obtain credit ratings from outside agencies such as Standard and Poors, Moodys or Fitch. Larger companies are more likely to use derivatives to change the maturity profile of debt than smaller companies, although there is still a tendency for both sizes of company to use them. Visibly, one of the largest differences in responses between

Table 5.19: Differences between large and small companies: Questionnaire A

	Small		*Large*		
Description	*No.*	*Mean*	*No.*	*Mean*	*Significance*
Yield curves predict future rates	38	2.71	41	3.17	0.023
The zero-coupon yield curve is useful	36	2.75	41	2.27	0.001
Floating-rate finance results in cheaper funding	38	3.13	41	2.61	0.042
Nearing covenants means managing the balance(s)	37	2.83	41	2.10	0.001
Bond market is cheaper than the bank market	38	3.26	41	2.66	0.014
Options will be used more under IAS 39	26	3.15	35	3.82	0.000
Swaptions will be used more under IAS 39	25	3.28	32	3.91	0.000

large and small companies is that of bond versus bank financing; smaller companies are much less likely to have bond financing than their larger counterparts. The lack of bond financing for smaller companies is probably also reflected in the absence of a credit rating for these firms. Moreover, the high costs and the need for specialist assistance with bond financing may also be a deterrent for smaller firms.

The currency of borrowing for smaller firms is also more likely to be in sterling than other currencies, again reflecting the fact that larger companies probably have greater access to the capital markets than smaller companies. However, larger companies often borrow and swap the proceeds, thus the currency of borrowing after swaps is possibly similar to that of the smaller companies, but the larger companies have the resources to take advantage of any arbitrage opportunities as these windows appear. Larger companies also appear to have the resources to manage interest rates on an internal basis without always resorting to the external markets.

The establishment of a focused treasury department in larger organisations also possibly explains why larger companies are able to take apart banks' packages, as they have the necessary specialist skills and resources. As a result, these companies are more fussy about the credit rating of the banks that they deal with.

The largest difference between the two categories of company is that larger firms are more likely to use exotic derivatives; again this may be because of the existence of dedicated treasury departments. The contrast in the mean response of small companies, at 4.65 (never use), and large companies of 1.24 (always use), is outstanding. Larger companies also use swaps more, but both only rarely appear to use swaptions, although again larger companies are more likely to use them.

Tables 5.19 and 5.20 report the differences between the two categories of company for Questionnaire A and Questionnaire B, respectively, where there were unique questions to both. The main point to emerge from these tables is that larger companies generally have stronger views about factors that affect IRR management than smaller companies.

Table 5.20: Differences between large and small companies: Questionnaire B

Description	Small No.	Small Mean	Large No.	Large Mean	Significance
Euro currency interest rate falls	47	2.77	32	2.91	0.019
Euro currency interest rate rises	46	2.78	32	2.16	0.011
Are borrowings swapped?	45	1.93	30	1.33	0.000
Is gap analysis used?	38	4.37	28	3.39	0.008
Is stress-testing used?	39	4.00	27	3.19	0.019

5.13 Summary

This chapter has examined the responses to a questionnaire survey that was posted in May and June 2003. The findings from the questionnaire survey support the findings from the interviews and the prior literature that was discussed in Chapter 2. Interest rate management appears to be based on a disbelief of efficient markets, where it is effective to adopt risk-averse strategies to manage an uncertain economic future (Froot, Scharfstein and Stein, 1993). Risk management practices appear to increase with increasing financial distress, whereby derivatives usage increases with gearing, low interest cover and low liquidity (Berkman and Bradbury, 1996; Berkman *et al.*, 1997b). Interest rate risk management is also carried out to hedge against volatile earnings, reduce the variability of cash flows and to manage the balance sheet (Bodnar, Hayt and Marston, 1996).

When respondents were asked about factors that affect their risk management there was agreement with the findings of Ross (2002) who indicated that with a positive yield curve it cost more to borrow long, and Douche (2002) who suggested that it was better to borrow floating if the treasurer expected rates to drop more than the yield curve suggested, but that if rates were expected to rise, it was better to fix as much as possible.

Foulkes (2002) stated that IAS 39 would cause a great deal of concern to treasurers, and this survey appeared to agree with that observation; treasurers from both the interviews and questionnaire were clearly apprehensive about the introduction of

IAS 39 in 2005. Also in agreement with the interviews, the survey found that the monitoring and control over treasury operations were inadequate, and as Mansell (2000) indicated, failings at Board level could have serious consequences for a company.

Overall, the findings reveal that there were a number of common themes amongst the respondents, but that there were also some important differences. Analyses of the data revealed that IRR management was of more importance to larger firms than smaller firms, that these larger firms tended to have dedicated treasury departments to manage their risk and thus larger firms were able to use more sophisticated products to manage their risk. However, risk management practices could be improved in some organisations, especially with regard to monitoring and control and the corporate governance implications of running a derivatives hedging programme.

6

Summary and Conclusions

This Page is Intentionally Left Blank

6.1 Introduction

This study has investigated the IRR management practices of UK companies. In particular, ten companies were visited and a postal questionnaire survey was conducted to examine the nine research questions outlined in Chapter 2. The findings for each of these key questions are discussed in this chapter, together with the policy implications of the findings.

6.2 The importance of interest rate risk

The findings from the interviews and the analysis of the questionnaire survey highlighted the fact that IRR management is of importance to UK firms. However, it appeared to be of more concern to larger companies than to smaller companies. Smaller companies possibly have more pressing needs such as strategy implementation, establishing a loyal customer base and sourcing raw materials rather than fine-tuning the management of financial risk.

6.3 The active management of interest rate risk and the establishment of policy

Most respondents to the survey had a formal Financial Risk Management Policy document. This generally detailed the amount of funding that should be fixed, with ranges set both by currency and for different periods out into the future. However, smaller companies were less likely to have formalised their IRR management policy to the same extent as larger companies. The interviews echoed this finding, revealing a variety of practices and policies.

6.4 The importance of interest rate risk to companies with different equity, funding and gearing structures

Most companies were more likely to fix the interest rates on their funding in the short term, but this tapered away as the time horizon extended into the future. The funding was usually through the banks, with only about a quarter of non-equity financing being raised through the issue of bonds. The term of the debt raised was generally medium term, from about four to seven years. Most funds were raised in either Sterling or Dollars, indicating that the US Dollar was still of major importance to UK firms. Raising finance in Euros was not so popular, and may reflect the hostility to the Euro within the UK or, alternatively, the fact that the UK is not in the Euro zone. Further, highly geared companies, close to covenant restrictions, were more likely to have fixed-rate finance in their debt structure.

6.5 Factors affecting interest rate risk

There were a number of views about the factors that influenced IRR policy. For example, companies with operations overseas were more likely to raise finance in those same foreign currencies. In analysing the questionnaire responses, there were certain themes that were evident: the yield curve and the zero-coupon yield curve were important; covenants influenced IRR management; floating-rate finance was cheaper than fixed-rate finance; and analysts' forecasts were poor. Respondents also appeared to lack faith in the yield curve. The interviews strongly supported these findings, and interviewees were consistent in the view that floating-rate finance in the capital structure resulted in greater earnings volatility.

There were only three factors that appeared to be important in explaining why companies attempted to manage their IRR: (i) to manage reported profits; (ii) to protect shareholder funds; and (iii) where the interest charge to EBIT/EBITDA was significant. Surprisingly, factors such as a high dividend payout ratio or poor financial ratios did not appear to impact on UK companies' IRR management decisions. However, the results from a principal components analysis suggested that all the factors could be distilled into just six: (i) financial distress proxies; (ii) tax incentives; (iii) business strategy; (iv) managing the bottom line; (v) covenants; and (vi) future opportunities.

6.6 Interest rate risk versus exchange rate risk

The questionnaire respondents were asked to state the importance of certain economic factors in assessing the importance of IRR and exchange rate risk. Unsurprisingly, UK economic indicators appeared to be the most important to the UK companies in this study. In addition, a principal components analysis revealed that interest rate factors to some extent dominated exchange rate factors as the data were crystallised into seven factors: (i) US Dollar and other currency interest rate changes; (ii) inflation and deflation; (iii) the Euro currency interest rate and exchange rate; (iv) the UK base rate; (v) the Euro and other currency interest rates; (vi) inflation; and (vii) oil price decreases.

6.7 Forecasting

When determining their interest rate policy, UK companies appeared to review the direction of interest rates and the magnitude of interest rate changes, but were ambivalent about GDP and industry trends. Inflation and deflationary indicators were also important, but not to the same extent as interest rates. The interviewees used a variety of external forecasts including those offered by banks, economists and analysts, as well as information service providers such as Bloomberg and Reuters.

6.8 The use of derivatives and the use of interest rate swaps

The prior literature has indicated that companies actively use derivative products to manage their IRR and that interest rate swaps are extremely important for IRR management (Helliar, 1997). The results of this study confirmed this trend that interest rate swaps were vital to effective IRR management. The findings also confirmed the results from previous studies which have suggested that companies did not like using exchange-traded products such as futures (Bodnar *et al.*, 1995). This finding resulted from either Boards of Directors prohibiting their use or because simpler or cheaper products offered the required functionality.

6.9 Corporate governance: Monitoring, reporting and control

The one disturbing finding of this study was that corporate governance issues surrounding the use of derivatives by UK companies probably still have some way to go to meet stakeholders' requirements. In particular, the lack of involvement of audit committees in financial risk management and the *ad hoc* nature of the monitoring of risk management by the Board of Directors was disturbing. Hopefully, as corporate governance issues increasingly make the headlines, Audit Committees, Boards of Directors and non-executive directors will increasingly play a larger part in the financial risk management of companies.

6.10 International accounting standards

The arrival of IAS 39 in 2005 will undoubtedly change the IRR management policies of UK firms. The respondents to the survey and the interviewees were all clear that IAS 39 might have far-reaching consequences for the use of derivative products. In particular, the use of options and exchange-traded products were likely to decrease·as companies tried to improve their practices to meet the onerous 'hedge accounting' rules and 'effectiveness' rules. Clearly, treasurers were concerned about the implications of complying with the provisions of IAS 39 for their future IRR management strategies.

6.11 Policy implications

This study has elicited the views and perceptions of a number of financial managers within UK companies. These views obviously reflect only the perceptions of those that participated in the study. However, a number of key issues have been highlighted in this investigation.

- Interest rate risk management is important to UK companies, and this is especially so for firms that have loan covenants in place. Thus, the decision of the Bank of England to raise, lower or maintain interest rates at its regular Monetary Policy Committee meetings has a major affect on UK industry;
- Many UK companies base their IRR management policy upon the shape of the current yield curve, projections of interest rates changes in the future, and the spreads between different credit ratings. Clearly, any surprise to the financial markets,

such as base-rate changes that do not reflect market sentiment, can have major consequences for many UK companies;

- The implementation of IAS 39 in 2005 by all EU countries may have unanticipated consequences on the risk management behaviour of UK firms and on financial markets. The reduction in the use of options and exchange-traded products may see the loss of more jobs in the financial services sector and may result in less efficient IRR management within companies;
- Corporate governance issues relating to financial risk management need to be improved to ensure that financial disasters such as Enron, Barings and Allied Irish Bank do not occur again;
- The continued training of managers about IRRM within organisations is imperative, to ensure that organisations are following best practice and are aware of the implications of their actions in a broader setting;
- The improvement in the basic training about IRR management in small firms may improve the economic performance of the UK as a whole. Arguably, smaller firms may suffer more from adverse movements in interest rates than their larger counterparts, which may be better placed to absorb any adverse effects. However, these smaller firms do not have the specialist skills needed to manage IRR management effectively, and as a result, many small businesses may suffer financial distress and have to close.

In summary, IRR management is of vital importance to UK companies, and the effective management of IRR should be of major concern to accountants, treasurers, regulators and governments.

This Page is Intentionally Left Blank

References

This Page is Intentionally Left Blank

Accountancy Age (1992), 'The Swaps Fiasco', September, p. 3.

Accounting Standards Board (1998), *Financial Reporting Standard 13: Derivatives and Other Financial Instruments – Disclosures*, September.

Accounting Standards Board (2002a), *Financial Reporting Exposure Draft 23: Financial Instruments – Hedge Accounting*, May.

Accounting Standards Board (2002b), *Financial Reporting Exposure Draft 30: Financial Instruments – Disclosure and Presentation, Recognition and Measurement*, June.

Accounting Standards Board (2002c), *Financial Reporting Standard 13: Derivatives and Other Financial Instruments – Disclosures*, September.

Adedeji, A. and Baker, C.R. (1999), 'Financial Reporting of Derivatives Before FRS 13', *Derivatives Use, Trading and Regulation*, Vol. 5, No. 1, pp. 51–62.

Ankrom, R.K. (1974), 'Top-Level Approach to the Foreign Exchange Problem', *Harvard Business Review*, July–August, pp. 79–90.

Awty, T. (2001), 'Countdown to New Standards has Started', *The Times*, Thursday, May 31.

Bank of England (1995), 'Statistical Information about Derivatives Markets', *Bank of England Quarterly Bulletin*, May.

Bank of England (2001), 'The Foreign Exchange and Over-the-counter Derivatives Markets in the United Kingdom', *Bank of England Quarterly Bulletin*, Winter, pp. 417–430.

Bank of England (2002), 'The Foreign Exchange and Over-the-counter Derivatives Markets in the United Kingdom', *Bank of England Quarterly Bulletin*, Spring.

Bartram, S. (2002), 'The Interest Rate Exposure of Non-Financial Corporations', *European Finance Review*, Vol. 6, pp. 101–125.

Batten, J., Mellor, R. and Wan, V. (1994), 'Interest Rate Risk Management Practices and Products Used by Australian Firms', *Research in International Business and Finance*, IIB, pp. 183–199.

Belk, P. and Glaum, M. (1990), 'The Management of Foreign Exchange Risk in UK Multinationals: An Empirical Investigation', *Accounting and Business Research*, Vol. 21, 81, pp. 3–13.

Bensten, G.J. and Hartgraves, A.L. (2002), 'Enron: What Happened and What We can Learn from it?', *Journal of Accounting and Public Policy*, Summer, Vol. 21, No. 2, pp. 105–127.

Berkman, H. and Bradbury, M.E. (1996), 'Empirical Evidence on the Corporate use of Derivatives', *Financial Management*, Vol. 25, No. 2, pp. 5–13.

Berkman, H., Bradbury, M.E., Hancock, P. and Innes, C. (1997a), 'An Analysis of Disclosures of Derivatives Financial Instruments in Australia and New Zealand', *Accounting Forum*, Vol. 21, No. 2, September, pp. 207–228.

Berkman, H., Bradbury, M.E. and Magan, S. (1997b), 'An International Comparison of Derivatives Use', *Financial Management*, Vol. 26, No. 4, Winter, pp. 69–73.

Bernstein, P.L. (1996), *Against the Gods: The Remarkable Story of Risk*, John Wiley & Sons, New York.

Bircher, P. (1999), 'FRS 13: Problems and More Problems', *Accountancy*, February, p. 86.

Block, S. and Gallagher, T. (1986), 'The Use of Interest Rate Futures and Options by Corporate Financial Managers', *Financial Management*, Vol. 15, No. 3, pp. 73–78.

Bodnar, G.M. and Gebhardt, G. (1998), 'Derivatives Usage in Risk Management by U.S. and German Non-Financial Firms: A Comparative Survey', *National Bureau of Economic Research*, Working Paper, No. 6705.

Bodnar, G.M., Hayt, G.S., Marston, R.C. and Smithson, C.W. (1995), 'Wharton Survey of Derivatives Usage by U.S. Non-Financial Firms', *Financial Management*, Vol. 24, No. 2, pp. 104–114.

Bodnar, G.M., Hayt, G.S. and Marston, R.C. (1996), '1995 Wharton Survey of Derivatives Usage by US Non-Financial Firms', *Financial Management*, Vol. 25, No. 4, pp. 113–133.

Bodnar, G.M., Hayt, G.S. and Marston, R.C. (1998), '1998 Wharton Survey of Derivatives Usage by US Non-Financial Firms', *Financial Management*, Vol. 4, No. 2, pp. 104–114.

Brigham, E.F. and Gapenski, L.C. (1994), *Financial Management Theory and Practice*, The Dryden Press, London, 7th edition.

Buckley, A. (2000), *Multinational Finance*, Pearson Education, Harlow, 4th edition.

Burgess, A. (2003), ' "Risk" and "Life" – Four Letter Words', *The Treasurer*, May, pp. 32–33.

Burton, B.M., Helliar, C.V. and Power, D.M. (2003), *A Behavioural Finance Perspective on IPOs and SEOs*, ACCA Research Monograph, London.

Business Week (1994), 'Managing Risk', October 31.

Cadbury, S.A. (1992), *Report of the Committee on the Financial Aspects of Corporate Governance*, Gee & Co. Ltd, London.

Chacko, G., Tufano, P. and Verter, G. (2001), 'Cephalon Inc. Taking Risk Management Theory Seriously', *Journal of Financial Economics*, Vol. 60, No. 2/3, pp. 449–485.

Chew, L. (1996), *Managing Derivative Risks: The Use and Abuse of Leverage*, John Wiley & Sons, Chichester.

Cobb, I., Helliar, C.V. and Innes, J. (1995), 'Management Accounting Change in a Bank', *Management Accounting Research*, Vol. 6, pp. 155–175.

Creed, D. (2001), 'Fellows Debate Financial Instruments Accounting', *The Treasurer*, July/August, p. 24.

Crockett, A.D. (1996), 'The Changing Structure of Financial Institutions and Markets: A Central Bank Perspective', in (eds) Bruni, F., Fair, D. and O'Brien, R., *Risk Management in Volatile Financial Markets*, Kluwer Academic Publishers, Dordrecht.

Davis, E., Coates, J., Collier, P. and Longden, S. (1991), *Currency Risk Management in MNCs*, Prentice-Hall.

De Marzo, P. and Duffie, D. (1995), 'Corporate Incentives for Hedging and Hedge Accounting', *Review of Financial Studies*, Vol. 8, pp. 743–772.

Dhanani, A. (2001), *Foreign Exchange Risk Management: An Empirical Investigation of Corporate Practices*, Unpublished PhD. Thesis, University of Wales, Cardiff.

Dhanani, A. (2003), 'Foreign Exchange Risk Management: A Case in the Mining Industry', *British Accounting Review*, Vol. 35, No. 1, pp. 35–63.

Di Paola, S. and Cattoor, O. (2000), 'Hedging and Internal Control Post-FAS 133', *The Treasurer*, November, pp. 35–38.

Dolde, W. (1993), 'The Trajectory of Corporate Financial Risk Management', *Journal of Applied Corporate Finance*, Fall, pp. 33–41.

Douche, N. (2002), 'Applying the Best Strategy', *The Treasurer*, pp. 51–52.

Dunne, T.M. and Helliar, C.V. (2002), 'The Ludwig Report: Implications for Corporate Governance', *Corporate Governance: The International Journal for Effective Board Performance*, Vol. 2, No. 3, pp. 26–31.

Dunne, T. and Helliar, C. (2004), 'Control of the Treasury Function', *Corporate Governance: International Journal of Business in Society*, Vol. 4, No. 2, pp. 34–43.

Dunne, T.M., Helliar, C.V., Mallin, C.A., Ow-Yong, K. and Power, D.M. (2003), 'The Introduction of Derivatives Reporting in the UK: A Content Analysis of FRS 13 Disclosures', Dundee Working Paper.

Dunne, T.M., Helliar, C.V., Mallin, C.A. and Ow-Yong, K. (2004), 'FRS 13 and Corporate Governance: A Fund Managers Perspective', *Qualitative Research in Accounting and Management*, Vol. 1, No. 2, pp. 17–42.

Financial Accounting Standards Board (1998), *Statement No. 133: Accounting for Derivative Instruments and Hedging Activities*, FASB.

Financial Accounting Standards Board (1999), *Statement No. 137: Accounting for Derivative Instruments and Hedging Activities—Deferral of the Effective Date of FASB Statement No. 133—An Amendment of FASB Statement No. 133*, FASB.

Financial Accounting Standards Board (2000), *Statement No. 138: Accounting for Derivative Instruments and Hedging Activities—An Amendment of FASB Statement No. 133*, FASB.

Finnerty, J.D. (1988), 'Financial Engineering in Corporate Finance: An Overview', *Financial Management*, Winter, pp. 14–33.

Finnerty, J.D. and Grant, D. (2002), 'Alternative Approaches to Testing Hedge Effectiveness Under SFAS NO. 133', *Accounting Horizons*, Vol. 16, No. 2, pp. 95–198.

Foulkes, A. (2002), 'New Accounting Rules Explained', *The Treasurer*, November, p. 23.

Friedman, L.A.F. and Joseph, M.S.J. (1993), 'A Blueprint for Controlling the Derivatives Business: Some Questions for Management', *Bank Accounting and Finance*, Vol. 6, No. 3, pp. 21–33.

Froot, K.A., Scharfstein, D.S. and Stein, J.C. (1993), 'Risk Management: Coordinating Corporate Investment and Financing Policies', *Journal of Finance*, Vol. XLVIII, No. 5, pp. 1629–1658.

Froot, K.A., Scharfstein, D.S. and Stein, J.C. (1994), 'A Framework for Risk Management', *Harvard Business Review*, November/December, pp. 91–102.

Galitz, L. (1994), *Financial Engineering: Tools and Techniques to Manage Financial Risk*, Pitman Publishing, London.

Gastineau, G. (1993), 'The Essential of Financial Risk Management', *Financial Analysts Journal*, September/October, 17–21.

Goodhart, C.A.E. (1996), 'Has Financial Risk Really Worsened?' in (eds) Bruni, F., Fair, D. and O'Brien, R., *Risk Management in Volatile Financial Markets*, Kluwer Academic Publishers, Dordrecht.

Grant, K. and Marshall, A. (1997), 'Large UK Companies and Derivatives', *European Financial Management*, 3, 2, pp. 191–208.

Hakkarainen, A., Kasanen, E. and Puttonen, V. (1997), 'Interest Rate Risk Management in Major Finnish Firms', *European Financial Management*, Vol. 3, No. 3, pp. 225–268.

Helliar, C. (1997), 'Uses of Interest Rate and Currency Swaps by Financial Managers', CIMA Monograph, London.

Helliar, C.V. (2004), 'Reasons for the Use of Interest Rate and Currency Swaps by UK Companies', *Journal of Applied Accounting Research*, Vol. 7, No. 1 (forthcoming).

Helliar, C.V. and Dunne, T.M. (2004), 'Control of the Treasury Function', *Corporate Governance: International Journal of Business in Society*, Vol. 4, No. 2, pp. 34–43.

Helliar, C.V., Lonie, A.A., Power, D.M. and Sinclair, C.D. (2001), 'Managerial Attitudes to Risk', *The Institute of Chartered Accountants of Scotland Research Monograph*, Edinburgh, p. 98.

Helliar, C.V., Cobb, I. and Innes, J. (2002a), 'A Longitudinal Case Study of Management Accounting in a Bank', *British Accounting Review*, Vol. 34, No. 1, pp. 27–53.

Helliar, C.V., Lonie, A.A., Power, D.M. and Sinclair, C.D. (2002b), 'Scottish Accountants Attitudes to Risk', *International Journal of Accounting, Auditing and Taxation*, Vol. 11, No. 2, pp. 165–190.

Helliar, C., Dunne, T. and Moir, L. (2004), 'Derivatives Reporting in the UK: A Treasury Perspective on the Introduction of FRS 13, *Journal of Applied Accounting Research*, Vol. 7, No. 2, p. 134.

Hentschel and Kothari (1995), 'Life Insurance or Lottery. Are Corporations Managing or Taking Risks with Derivatives?', Plenary paper, BAA Conference, Bristol.

Hinks, G. (2001), 'Ignore FRS 13 at your Peril', *Accountancy Age*, April 19th, p. 5.

Hogan, W.P. (1997), 'Corporate Governance Lessons from Barings', *Abacus*, Vol. 33, No. 1, pp. 1–23.

Holland, J.B. (1993), *International Financial Management*, 2nd edition, Blackwell, Oxford.

Holmes, D.E.A. and Watson, H.D. (1995), 'Interest Rate Management Procedures of the Top 500 Quoted Companies', Working Paper, School of Financial Studies and Law, Sheffield Hallam University.

Horton, J. and Macve, R. (2000), '"Fair Value" for Financial Instruments: How Erasing Theory is Leading to Unworkable Global Accounting Standards for Performance Reporting', *Australian Accounting Review*, Vol. 11, No. 2, pp. 26–39.

Howton, S.D. and Perfect, S.B. (1998), 'Currency and Interest Rate Derivatives Use in Financial Firms', *Financial Management*, Vol. 27, No. 4, pp. 111–121.

Hussey, J. and Hussey, R. (1997), *Business Research*, Macmillan, London.

ICAEW (1997), *Financial Reporting of Risk – Proposals for a Statement of Business Risk*, December, ICAEW, London.

ICAEW (1999), 'Internal Control Working Party', *Internal Control: Guidance for Directors on the Combined Code*, Institute of Chartered Accountants in England and Wales, London.

Institute of Chartered Accountants in England and Wales (ICAEW) (2002), 'Risk Management Survey: How CFOs See their Role in Risk Management', *Management Quarterly*, January, pp. 34–35.

International Accounting Standards Committee (1998), *IAS 39, Financial Instruments: Recognition and Measurement*, IASC.

Joint Working Group of Standard Setters (1999), *Recommendations on Accounting for Financial Instruments and Similar Items*.

Jorion, P. (1995), *Big Bets Gone Bad: Derivatives and Bankruptcy in Orange County*, Academic Press, San Diego.

Knight, F.H. (1921), *Risk, Uncertainty and Profit*, Boston, Houghton Mifflin.

Leeson, N. (1996), '*Rogue Trader*', Little, Brown and Company, London.

Linsley, P. and Shrives, P. (2001), 'Truth or Dare', *Financial Management*, May, p. 40.

Mallin, C.A., Ow-Yong, K. and Reynolds, M. (2001), 'Derivatives Usage in UK Non-Financial Listed Companies', *The European Journal of Finance*, Vol. 7, No. 1, pp. 63–91.

Mansell, C. (2000), 'A Control Framework', *Financial Focus*, Issue 59.
Mansell, C. (2003), 'Hedging Revisited', *Finance and Management*, April, p. 14.
March, J.G. and Simon, H.A. (1958), *Organizations*, John Wiley & Sons Inc., New York.
Marshall, A.P. (2000), 'Foreign Exchange Risk Management in UK USA and Asia-Pacific Multinational Companies', *Journal of Multinational Financial Management*, Vol. 10, pp. 185–211.
Mayers, D. and Smith, C. (1982), 'On the Corporate Demand for Insurance', *Journal of Business*, Vol. 55, pp. 281–297.
McDonough, W.J. (1993), 'The Global Derivatives Market', *Federal Reserve Bank of New York, Quarterly Review*, September, pp. 1–5.
McIlwraith, R. and Dealy, N. (2000), 'Learning from Experience', *Accountancy*, February, pp. 88–90.
Mian, S.L. (1996), 'Evidence on Corporate Hedging Policy', *Journal of Financial and Quantitative Analysis*, Vol. 31, No. 3, pp. 419–439.
Modigliani, F. and Miller, M.H. (1958), 'The Cost of Capital, Corporation Finance and the Theory of Investment', *American Economic Review*, Vol. XLVIII, No. 3, June, pp. 261–297.
Moffet, M.H. and Karlsen, J.K. (1994), 'Managing Foreign Exchange Rate Economic Exposure', *Journal of International Financial Management and Accounting*, Vol. 5, No. 2, pp. 157–174.
Mortimer, S. (2003), 'Gaining the Right Exposure', *The Treasurer*, May, pp. 46–48.
Mueller, C. (2003), 'IAS 39: Prospects for Implementation Among European Corporations', http://www.gtnews.com/article4824.
Osterland, A. (2001), 'Life Under FAS 133', *CFO Magazine*, July 1st [http://www.cfo.com/printarticle/1,4580,0|83|AD|3906,00.html] (03/09/01).
Overdahl, J. and Schachter, B. (1995), 'Derivatives Regulation and Financial Management: Lessons from Gibson Greetings', *Financial Management*, Spring, pp. 68–78.
Phillips, A.L. (1995), '1995 Derivatives Practices and Instruments Survey', *Financial Management*, Vol. 24, No. 2, pp. 115–125.
Prevost, A.K., Rose, L.C. and Miller, G. (2000), 'Derivatives Usage and Financial Risk Management in Large and Small Economies: A Comparative Analysis', *Journal of Business Finance & Accounting*, Vol. 27, No. 5 and 6, June/July, pp. 733–759.

Raeburn, R. and Boyle, J. (2002), 'Forget the FRED', *Accountancy*, October, p. 94.

Raeburn, R. and Gunson, T. (2003), 'Creating Value with a Financial: Risk Framework', *Management Quarterly*, pp. 21–26.

Rawls, S.W. and Smithson, C.W. (1990), 'Strategic Risk Management', *Continental Bank Journal of Applied Corporate Finance*, Vol. 1, pp. 59–72.

Revsine, L. (2002), 'Euron: Sad but Inevitable', *Journal of Accounting and Public Policy*, Vol. 21, pp. 137–146.

Ross, D. (2002), 'No Perfect Answer', *Accountancy*, August, p. 87.

Smith, C. and Stulz, R.M. (1985), 'The Determinants of Firms' Hedging Policies', *Journal of Financial and Quantitative Analysis*, Vol. 20, pp. 391–405.

Stulz, R.M. (1984), 'Optimal Hedging Policies', *Journal of Financial and Quantitative Analysis*, Vol. 16, pp. 302–317.

Titman, S. (2002), 'The Modigliani and Miller Theorem and the Integration of Financial Markets', *Financial Management*, Spring, pp. 101–115.

Turnbull, N. (1999), *Corporate Guidance for Internal Control*, Gee & Co. Ltd, London.

Wallace, R.S.O. and Mellor, C.J. (1988), 'Non-Response Bias in Mail Accounting Surveys: A Pedagogical Note', *British Accounting Review*, Vol. 20, pp. 131–139.

Index

This Page is Intentionally Left Blank

Printed in Dunstable, United Kingdom

91900957R00078